FRESH START FOR MOMS

Lord bless you!
+
Soli de gloria!
♡ Val

FRESH START

for moms

VALERIE WOERNER

TYNDALE
MOMENTUM®

The nonfiction imprint of
Tyndale House Publishers, Inc.

Visit Tyndale online at www.tyndale.com.

Visit Tyndale Momentum online at www.tyndalemomentum.com.

Visit the author at www.valmariepaper.com.

TYNDALE, *Tyndale Momentum*, and Tyndale's quill logo are registered trademarks of Tyndale House Publishers, Inc. The Tyndale Momentum logo is a trademark of Tyndale House Publishers, Inc. Tyndale Momentum is the nonfiction imprint of Tyndale House Publishers, Inc., Carol Stream, Illinois.

Fresh Start for Moms: A 31-Day Devotional Journal to Renew Your Joy

Copyright © 2019 by Valerie Woerner. All rights reserved.

Custom hand-lettering by Rachel Jacobson. Copyright © Tyndale House Publishers, Inc. All rights reserved.

Author photo by Whitney Marie Photography, copyright © 2018. All rights reserved.

Designed by Julie Chen

Edited by Stephanie Rische

Published in association with Folio Literary Management, LLC, 630 9th Avenue, Suite 1101, New York, NY 10036.

Unless otherwise indicated, all Scripture quotations are taken from the *Holy Bible*, New Living Translation, copyright © 1996, 2004, 2015 by Tyndale House Foundation. Used by permission of Tyndale House Publishers, Inc., Carol Stream, Illinois 60188. All rights reserved.

Scripture quotations marked AMP are taken from the Amplified® Bible, copyright © 2015 by The Lockman Foundation. Used by permission. www.Lockman.org.

Scripture quotations marked NIV are taken from the Holy Bible, *New International Version*,® *NIV*.® Copyright © 1973, 1978, 1984, 2011 by Biblica, Inc.® Used by permission. All rights reserved worldwide.

Scripture quotations marked MSG are taken from *THE MESSAGE*, copyright © 1993, 1994, 1995, 1996, 2000, 2001, 2002 by Eugene H. Peterson. Used by permission of NavPress. All rights reserved. Represented by Tyndale House Publishers, Inc.

Scripture quotations marked ESV are taken from *The Holy Bible*, English Standard Version® (ESV®), copyright © 2001 by Crossway, a publishing ministry of Good News Publishers. Used by permission. All rights reserved.

Scripture quotations marked NASB are taken from the New American Standard Bible,® copyright © 1960, 1962, 1963, 1968, 1971, 1972, 1973, 1975, 1977, 1995 by The Lockman Foundation. Used by permission.

For information about special discounts for bulk purchases, please contact Tyndale House Publishers at csresponse@tyndale.com, or call 1-800-323-9400.

ISBN 978-1-4964-3534-7

Printed in China

25   24   23   22   21   20   19
7   6   5   4   3   2   1

CONTENTS

IT'S TIME FOR A
FRESH START

ARE YOU FEELING WEARY, grumpy, impatient, or just plain bored on this journey of motherhood? If so, I'm in the trenches with you right now. I know these feelings all too well:

- that ache that sets in before your eyes even open and your toes hit the floor
- that thought that the day will bring you more than you can possibly handle
- that dread that today holds nothing more than your mundane routine

In a split second, before you even get out of bed, you've decided whether you will conquer your day or simply surrender to it.

I'm a mom to two girls, Vivi (four) and Vana (two), so I'm still early on my journey of motherhood. I have a whole lot to learn and many trials ahead, but one thing I know for certain is that God has burdened me with a desire to face whatever is to come with a fresh perspective. This doesn't come naturally for me—I'm someone with a tendency toward melancholy—so this God-sized perspective is something I have to fight for.

My prayer is that over the next thirty-one days, you will be refreshed and empowered in the knowledge that motherhood is so much more than making it through the day or hobbling through on caffeine and chocolate. You can kneel in front of a tantrum-throwing two-year-old or stand firmly in front of a disengaged teen and patiently speak truth and love in a way that trains their hearts to look more like Jesus. You can feel satisfied when you notice the sweat on your brow that comes from loving your family well. You can snuggle a baby way past bedtime and be grateful for the blessing of the extra time instead of feeling like it's ruining your plans.

You can do all this not because I say so but because God does.

I wrote this devotional for every mom who is craving a fresh start—not just in her day but in her approach to motherhood. We don't have to wake up with that ache or already-exhausted feeling. We can wake up with contagious joy and a peace that will change our homes—and us.

Your fresh start is here, momma! Dive in with me!

HOW TO USE THIS JOURNAL

I know how busy you are, and I don't want to waste your time with fluff or things that won't really serve you. My goal is not to create another thing you must do or something that will overwhelm your already-full life. My desire is to create a habit of thinking differently. Sometimes just the thought of a long-term commitment can prompt us to give up before we start. So, momma, I've made this as practical as possible so that by the end of the month, you will find that your thinking has been transformed.

Each day consists of a devotional, an action step, a prayer, and several questions for each morning, as well as a few reflection questions to end your day. To get the most out of the next thirty-one days, here's what I recommend committing to:

1. Set aside fifteen to twenty minutes in the morning and five to ten minutes at night for the next thirty-one days.
2. Read the devotional, follow the action step, and pray the prayer at the end.
3. Go through the morning questions before your day gets started.
4. As you climb into bed, make a nightly ritual of answering the evening questions.
5. You can use the page called "My Prayer" to journal your reflections and prayers at the end of the day.

I know there are so many other demands and obligations on your plate, but you need to know that you are valuable and this is worth your time. Prioritize this, fit it into your schedule, and process each day's reading fully so it can take root in your mind. This isn't urgent like getting the kids to school or putting dinner on the table, but it's important, so I'm challenging you to really make the most of this! If you do, you will start to see that you don't have to live in overwhelmed mode. You will start to experience more moments that make you love motherhood instead of just trying to get through the day. I can't promise you a quiet and pristine house (or kids!), but I can promise you a fresh start in the way you respond to the challenges, which fortunately makes all the difference in the world.

Valerie Woe

SPRING 2019

GETTING A HEALTHY GLOW

AT THE RIPE AGE of thirty-three, I'm starting to notice the crater-sized pores on my face, the stray facial hairs, and the ruddy complexion. Yesterday I found a hair that was literally an inch long coming from my forehead! How? When I look in the mirror, I feel too young to feel this old. I get overwhelmed by the idea that this skin isn't getting any better, and the rate of deterioration is only going to accelerate over the next thirty-three-plus years. But before I take a nosedive into a sea of miracle creams, I'd like to spend some time in the book of Exodus, where we can learn an unexpected lesson in beauty from Moses. I know. It seems like I'm reaching on this one, but stay with me. That old guy with skin that was no doubt windburned and dry from decades in the desert knew a thing or two about getting a healthy glow.

I've always been captivated by Moses and his relationship with the Lord. The conversations he had with God and the things God said about him carry a lot of relevance for us today. I'm continually amazed by the intimacy he had with the Lord—something I wouldn't typically expect for someone in the Old Testament. Over and over in Scripture we see Moses coming to the Lord in prayer, and we see God responding. God saved the Israelites time and time again, he healed Moses' sister Miriam, and he turned away his wrath—all because Moses asked him to.

Perhaps most amazing of all, Moses got to go on a mountaintop and speak face-to-face with God. Here's what happened afterward: "The Israelites would see the face of Moses, how his skin shone [with a unique radiance]. So Moses put the veil on his face again until he went in to speak with God" (Exodus 34:35, AMP).

Y'all, I just love this! I want that healthy glow—the kind that comes from spending time in the Lord's presence. I want to invest my time doing something that literally changes my countenance. I want to glow—not the glow that comes from too much time in front of my cell phone screen, but the one that comes from staring into the face of God as I read his Word and pray.

As much as I'd love smooth, porcelain skin, that desire starts to wane as I compare it to the potential for a heavenly glow that no manufactured product could create. And it's not just Moses who got to experience this: "The Lord is the Spirit, and wherever the Spirit of the Lord is, there is freedom. So all of us who have had that veil removed can see and reflect the glory of the Lord. And the Lord—who is the Spirit—makes us more and more like him as we are changed into his glorious image" (2 Corinthians 3:17-18). As I read these words, my heart aches with excitement over the idea that this can be true of me— that I, too, could reflect the glory of the Lord.

The real glow is found in the presence of the Lord, so keep running back to him. Wake up each morning with him so that when you close your Bible or say "Amen," you walk out fresh faced and ready to tackle the day.

I want my kids to notice a difference in me after I pray and read the Word, not just when I slap on a little lipstick and mascara. I want to walk away different. Spending time with God has the power to do that. I just have to apply his Word to my life.

Here's one final encouragement as you ponder what it means to glow as you spend time in God's Word and in prayer: "Don't assume that you know it all. Run to GOD! Run from evil! Your body will glow with health, your very bones will vibrate with life!" (Proverbs 3:7-8, MSG).

The presence of the Lord changes us. It brings life to our aching bones and aging faces, and it can change our countenance more than any magical elixir.

ACTION STEP

Commit to meeting with the Lord each morning, even if it's just for a few minutes, before you meet with anyone else. Let him shine on you so that you can walk out of your room or your house different than you were before.

PRAYER

Father, I want beautiful skin, but I want you more. This is my prayer: that I would clamor for time with you more than I strive to perfect my outside. The radiance that shines in me when I am in your presence is more beautiful than anything I could imagine. Help me to remember that. In Jesus' name, amen.

MORNING QUESTIONS

TAKEAWAY TODAY | *Who in your life has a glow about them from spending time with Jesus?*

How can you spend some time today basking in the Lord's presence? You could put on worship music in the car or listen to Scripture while you're running errands.

DREADING TODAY | *Is there anything you're dreading today?*

REDEFINING TODAY | *If so, what is another way you can view that thing you're dreading?*

ASKING GOD TODAY | *What request are you bringing before the Lord today?*

EVENING QUESTIONS

REFLECTION | *Were there any moments today when you sensed that you had a "glow" as a result of spending time in God's presence?*

LITTLE VICTORIES | *Where did you see God show up even in small ways, reminding you that you aren't alone?*

WHITE FLAG MOMENTS | *When did you want to hide or escape today? It helps to recognize your toughest moments so you can figure out what's driving you there and conquer the temptation to check out.*

MEMORY OF THE DAY | *What do you want to relish and thank God for?*

MY PRAYER

OUR THREE ENEMIES

WE HAVE THREE ENEMIES, Tim Keller says. And contrary to what I sometimes assume, they don't go by the names of Tyler (my husband), Vivi, or Vana (my girls). Nope. My enemies are the world, the flesh, and the devil. Today, momma, we are suiting up so we can learn how to respond to the real enemies instead of devoting energy to battling those who are, in fact, on our teams.

Maybe you've had days when you feel like you are taking on the greatest evil that ever lived: a toddler who hasn't napped and is demanding dinner. Or maybe you've teamed up with your kids to feel like the victims of your husband, who got home late again.

Even the idea that we could see our kids or spouse as the enemy reveals that we have another enemy who is working aggressively to convince us that ripping our teammates apart is the way to feel better or get what we want. It isn't.

Let's talk specifics. Being aware of our real enemies and their usual tactics is the first step to defeating them.

Enemy #1: The world. Our world constantly lies to us about motherhood, and those lies can hold us back from enjoying the life God has graciously given us. We are currently living in enemy territory, and we can't get so comfortable that we start thinking this place is our home. When we do, the lies can seep in and defeat us. As it says in 1 John 5:19-20, "We know that we are children of God, and that the whole world is under the control of the evil one. We know also that the Son of God has come and has given us understanding, so that we may know him who is true. And we are in him who is true by being in his Son Jesus Christ" (NIV).

Enemy #2: The flesh. We were born sinners, and because of this, we don't have a natural bent toward holiness. We are constantly fighting against our flesh, which is wired to choose evil. As hopeless as that sounds, as believers we are overflowing with hope because the Holy Spirit is at work in us. But we have to know our natural bent so we don't trust every thought that comes to mind. Instead of going along with our natural tendencies, we need to set our minds on something better. Romans 8:5-6 says, "Those who live according to the flesh set their minds on the things of the flesh, but those who live according to the Spirit set their minds on the things of the Spirit. For to set the mind on the flesh is death, but to set the mind on the Spirit is life and peace" (ESV).

Enemy #3: The devil. The devil has not a single good plan for our lives. He is out to destroy us. If he's missed the chance to keep us enemies of God, he will at the very least try to keep us so busy and distracted that we won't recruit anyone to the Lord's side. Those distractions might come in the form of thinking of ourselves too much or even in the form of something good, like establishing our kids' healthy physical habits, but at the expense of neglecting their hearts. John 10:10 says, "The thief comes only to steal and kill and destroy; I have come that they may have life, and have it to the full" (NIV).

The ally: God. Sometimes, as crazy as this might sound at first, we can treat God like the enemy. We balk at his direction. We assume we have a better plan. We get upset because life isn't going the way we'd hoped, and we assume it's because God has forgotten us or, worse, that he sees us but just doesn't care. That's when we need to remember that God sent his Son to die so that we could have life. Did you catch that? A *full* life. When our days get crazy, we have to run into the arms of God in full assurance that we are safe there, instead of running into the arms of the enemy.

ACTION STEP

The next time you feel like you are bracing for a fight, identify the real enemy. Is the enemy really your kid who is fighting bedtime, or is it the lie of the world that your comfort is most important and your demands should be met perfectly? Meditate on these verses today: Romans 8:1-11; Ephesians 6:12; and 1 Peter 5:8.

PRAYER

Father, I've been fighting the wrong enemies—and it's exhausting. Arm me with your truth. Help me to identify my real enemies, and help me to create a strong alliance in my family and with you. In Jesus' name, amen.

MORNING QUESTIONS

TAKEAWAY TODAY | *Who do you tend to assume your enemies are?*

Which real enemy (the world, the flesh, or the devil) trips you up the most?

DREADING TODAY | *Is there anything you're dreading today?*

REDEFINING TODAY | *If so, what is another way you can view that thing you're dreading?*

ASKING GOD TODAY | *What request are you bringing before the Lord today?*

EVENING QUESTIONS

REFLECTION | *Were there any moments today when you sensed that God was your ally?*

LITTLE VICTORIES | *Where did you see God show up even in small ways, reminding you that you aren't alone?*

WHITE FLAG MOMENTS | *When did you want to hide or escape today?*

MEMORY OF THE DAY | *What do you want to relish and thank God for?*

MY PRAYER

THIS PRESENT GUILT

As I PLOPPED DOWN in my favorite booth at the coffee shop with my green tea and added collagen (that's to impress you health nuts) and began to write, I did this thing that I find myself doing most workdays. I got all sentimental about my girls and watched at least one video of them on my phone before I started my work. That's cute, right?

But here's what it actually looked like: I pictured the blissful fun I should have been having with them at that moment and immediately felt guilty for working instead of spending time with them. I chastised myself for being a distracted mom and wondered if I should go home so I could let the Lord use me to change their little lives. The result was a distracted author.

This is just one of the ways Satan uses false guilt to hamper what God wants to do through us. We can spend all our time thinking we should be in the utopian version of whatever we're missing out on. On this occasion, though, as I was sitting in front of my computer wishing I was with my girls, I thought about the reality. I pictured my girls in the car with me without all the beautiful, noise-reducing Instagram filters. And guess what I was doing? I was wishing I had time to think and write! It's absolute madness, right? I was doing the very thing I wanted to be doing in that moment that I thought I wanted right now. Here's another way of putting it: the grass is always greener on the other side, while the guilt is always heavier on my side.

It's true that there's healthy guilt that comes from conviction over sin. But this guilt over not being everywhere at once is not based on reality. We cannot be physically present for our children every moment of every day. If we try to hold ourselves to this standard, the irony is that we will live consumed (and distracted) by our guilt for not spending enough time with our kids.

So yes, you might have some real issues to bring to the Lord about areas of sin and things you know you need to change. But let's not amplify that by feeling guilty over made-up things. Instead, let's live in the freedom the Cross offers so we can actually enjoy those kids we feel guilty for not enjoying more.

Here's how this works in my world, practically speaking. I set aside the first hour after the girls wake up and the first hour after nap time as no-phone time. I make sure I am really present, and I ask them lots of questions. I make sure to fill their tanks. Normally that hour prepares my heart for a more present day, and if there are moments I just have to get the dishes done or do some work while they play on the floor by themselves, I don't need to feel guilty about it.

I used to get kind of mad about how prevalent the message of grace is in the church. I used to think grace meant a free pass to sin. But that's not real grace. When we truly understand grace, it frees us up to live a life of obedience. Grace doesn't replace obedience; it energizes and propels our obedience. As we seek to be more present, we need to cling to this grace instead of living under a cloud of false guilt.

Romans 8:1-2 says, "There is now no condemnation for those who are in Christ Jesus, because through Christ Jesus the law of the Spirit who gives life has set you free from the law of sin and death" (NIV). I want to live each day as if I believe this to be true. Let's not let our guilt about not being more present with our kids become another distraction from being present with them. May the grace of God propel us forward into obedience and into undistracted moments with our kids—without all the residue of guilt.

ACTION STEP

Choose one hour today to be present with your kids. You can cook together or enjoy a meal around the table, distraction free. If your kids are younger, you may want to start the time by reading books together. If you have older children, you might want to try a board game or card game.

PRAYER

Father, I long to be present with my children, but in doing so, I carry a weight of guilt that you never asked me to carry. Show me how to walk in the freedom that you have already paid for. Let your grace propel me forward in obedience. In Jesus' name, amen.

MORNING QUESTIONS

TAKEAWAY TODAY | *When are you most likely to feel a sense of false guilt?*

When is it hardest for you to be present (e.g., with your children, with your spouse, at work)?

DREADING TODAY | *Is there anything you're dreading today?*

REDEFINING TODAY | *If so, what is another way you can view that thing you're dreading?*

ASKING GOD TODAY | *What request are you bringing before the Lord today?*

EVENING QUESTIONS

REFLECTION | *Were you able to spend some time being fully present with your children? What went well and what was challenging about that time?*

LITTLE VICTORIES | *Where did you see God show up even in small ways, reminding you that you aren't alone?*

WHITE FLAG MOMENTS | *When did you want to hide or escape today?*

MEMORY OF THE DAY | *What do you want to relish and thank God for?*

MY PRAYER

AN INCOMPREHENSIBLE PLAN

THERE IS ONE OVERARCHING TRUTH about God that has the potential to turn our attitudes around more quickly than anything else: God's ways are on a whole other level than ours. And there's an equally compelling truth about ourselves: we do not have all the facts.

I have to remind myself often of this second point, even if I like to think I have the most facts of anyone in my household. The level of vision that God has compared to mine is vast and thorough and extensive and every other word in the thesaurus that even comes close to all-knowing. Isaiah 55:8-9 gives us this perspective: "My thoughts are not your thoughts, neither are your ways my ways, declares the LORD. For as the heavens are higher than the earth, so are my ways higher than your ways and my thoughts than your thoughts" (ESV).

I love seeing this truth in action as we read about the Lord preparing Moses to go to Egypt and confront Pharaoh. Exodus 6:1 says, "Now you will see what I will do to Pharaoh. When he feels the force of my strong hand, he will let the people go. In fact, he will force them to leave his land!"

I can imagine how Moses must have heard that promise. If you were Moses, would you have expected *ten* plagues before Pharaoh finally threw the Israelites out of Egypt? I would have expected to do my little staff-into-serpent thing, then a little turning the Nile River into blood, and then—shazam—we'd be on our way. Moses heard the promise straight from God's mouth that he would deliver his people, but even he could be thrown off, assuming God had messed up or forgotten him. Why? Because like I mentioned earlier, God's ways are on a whole other level from ours.

This is why, in those moments when I've prayed for peace that passes all understanding (Philippians 4:7) or for joy to come in the morning (Psalm 30:5) and I'm still not seeing those promises materialize, I have to remember that I'm not seeing the full picture. We may never understand the big things that happen to us—like why our child was born with a heart defect—or the small things, for that matter—like why our kid won't sleep through the night. There are a lot of things we are not going to understand.

And when we encounter situations that are beyond our comprehension, we can rest knowing that it's okay not to understand. In fact, this is actually perfectly normal. And when we keep in mind how big our God is, we can respond to these unknowns without shocked faces or face-palm moments.

The next time you're tempted to shake your head in utter dismay at the way motherhood looks, remember God's perspective on your life. Just because you can't explain it doesn't mean it's not right on track. And even if you're following God's leading to adopt a child or start a business or stay at home for a season, it might still look messy at times.

In *None like Him*, Jen Wilkin says that God himself is incomprehensible. "This does not mean that he is unknowable, but that he is unable to be fully known."[1] Doesn't it stand to reason that his plans are incomprehensible as well, since they were created by an incomprehensible God? The unknown is scary, but when we start with the character of God, it can actually be exciting, too. The fact that we don't know all there is to know about God means there are more amazing things to learn about him. There isn't some dark, hidden closet—just more of the good stuff that drew us to him in the first place. In the face of unknown circumstances, I want the truth about who God is to crowd out the fear I feel or the desire I have to control the situation. I want to wake up excited to look for and find out just a little bit more about God each day.

ACTION STEP

Write down the craziest thing in your life that you don't understand right now. Then in a big, bold Sharpie, write over it, "I don't understand this, but God does."

PRAYER

Father, why? Some days, I feel that's all I have the strength to utter. And although I don't understand, and my lack of understanding frustrates me sometimes, help me to see the beauty in the incomprehensible. Remind me of your high-level view that can't possibly compare to mine. In Jesus' name, amen.

MORNING QUESTIONS

TAKEAWAY TODAY | *Think of an incomprehensible situation you have faced in the past. Does it make more sense in retrospect?*

What are some specific traits about God's character that you want to remember today?

DREADING TODAY | *Is there anything you're dreading today?*

REDEFINING TODAY | *If so, what is another way you can view that thing you're dreading?*

ASKING GOD TODAY | *What request are you bringing before the Lord today?*

EVENING QUESTIONS

REFLECTION | *What unknowns did you face today? How did you respond to these circumstances that were outside your control?*

LITTLE VICTORIES | *Where did you see God show up even in small ways, reminding you that you aren't alone?*

WHITE FLAG MOMENTS | *When did you want to hide or escape today?*

MEMORY OF THE DAY | *What do you want to relish and thank God for?*

MY PRAYER

BLINDSIDED

SOME DAYS I STILL get blindsided by the seemingly harmless lies the world tells us about motherhood. It happens often when I'm talking to another mom I don't know well. As I search for a common topic of conversation, one thing that rises to the top is our complaints—about our mutual unwashed hair or the minivan life. Despite all the wonderful things about motherhood, the complaints are often the loudest. And the reality is, this does a number on my view of motherhood.

If we are living like the world, we will miss out on the abundant motherhood God has for us. God's design means less yelling, more joy, less chaos, and fewer guilt-ridden moments—not to mention refreshment that the world cannot possibly offer us.

Romans 12:2 says, "Do not conform to the pattern of this world, but be transformed by the renewing of your mind. Then you will be able to test and approve what God's will is—his good, pleasing and perfect will" (NIV). The temptation to conform to the world isn't something new, as we can see from this passage.

In fact, this pressure is even older than the book of Romans. I'm talking Old Testament old.

We read about David's son Solomon in 1 Kings 11:1-2: "King Solomon loved many foreign women. . . . The LORD had clearly instructed the people of Israel, 'You must not marry them, because they will turn your hearts to their gods.' Yet Solomon insisted on loving them anyway."

I remember being shocked when my mom told me how Solomon had made some bad choices. I knew about his many wives but thought this was a cultural thing. How had I glossed over that major detail? Wasn't this the guy who chose wisdom over riches? The one who built the Temple? What happened? I went back and read his full story in the Bible, and suddenly it made sense. He conformed to the patterns of the world around him instead of renewing his mind in truth. He disobeyed the Lord and loved the women of the world, and as a result, his heart turned to their gods.

We can be good Bible-study girls, with our color-coding systems and our prayers organized in journals, but if we fail to protect our hearts, we will still take a wrong turn (which often starts with just a slight veer).

It's hard to guard our hearts against conforming to the world, because the world looks very normal. Hello! We've lived our entire existence here. It feels like home even though for the believer it's not.

What does it look like to stay vigilant and protect our hearts from the ways of the world? How do we let the truth in all that studying and reading we've done change the way we live? How do we stay alert when a lie comes prowling around dressed as a normal thought?

Proverbs 4:23 says, "Above all else, guard your heart, for everything you do flows from it" (NIV). I've heard this passage countless times. I know it inside and out. But one day as I read it, the urgency in the words hit me in a new way.

We live in a world that has instant and constant access to us. We have very few natural barriers for what comes in. TV shows, blog posts, everyday conversations, and social media in every form bombard us with what the world believes.

God's Word calls us to create proper barriers around our hearts and minds. This kind of guarding requires action on our part. If we sit back, the boundaries won't accidentally fall into place. The world has no interest in creating healthy limits for us. But the good news is we don't do it on our own. The Holy Spirit is at work in us and equips us to do what we could never accomplish on our own. Isn't it empowering to know that we don't have to be victims of this world? In God's strength, we are strong and capable enough to knock out whatever goes against his truth.

ACTION STEP

Evaluate what messages are coming in to your mind today. Which of these messages need to be stopped?

PRAYER

Father, thank you for equipping me to guard my heart well. Help me to remember that I do not have to be a victim of the world around me. Give me the courage to shut off access to the things that drag me down and separate me from you. In Jesus' name, amen.

MORNING QUESTIONS

TAKEAWAY TODAY | *When do you tend to have the most trouble guarding your heart (when you're on Instagram, when you're talking with friends, when you're watching Netflix, etc.)?*

Who can keep you accountable in setting up some boundaries against the world's input?

DREADING TODAY | *Is there anything you're dreading today?*

REDEFINING TODAY | *If so, what is another way you can view that thing you're dreading?*

ASKING GOD TODAY | *What request are you bringing before the Lord today?*

EVENING QUESTIONS

REFLECTION | *Were there any lies you noticed trying to creep into your mind today? How did you respond?*

LITTLE VICTORIES | *Where did you see God show up even in small ways, reminding you that you aren't alone?*

WHITE FLAG MOMENTS | *When did you want to hide or escape today?*

MEMORY OF THE DAY | *What do you want to relish and thank God for?*

MY PRAYER

LESSONS FROM MOM

I GREW UP A WORRIED little child, whether it was about a real situation I was dealing with or a problem I had worked up in my imagination. Whatever I was worried about, my mom's antidote was always the same: prayer.

Your ear hurts? Let's pray.
You're scared of a house fire after the fire department
    demonstration at school? Let's pray.
Your sister is being mean? Let's pray.

I grew up knowing that God cared about me and that I could turn to him for everything simply because that's what my mom lived out. Nothing was too small or too big for God. I would not be the woman I am today and I don't think I'd have the faith I have today without her influence.

But if you were thinking my mom was some picture-perfect mom who baked cookies every day, quoted a verse for every issue, and had a calm voice every time I did something dumb, you'd be wrong.

My mom taught me how to pray, but she also taught me how to cuss.

We never had any formal swearing lessons, but this Bible-ready prayer warrior also let words fly when she stubbed her toe, when something spilled, or when plans went haywire. I didn't escape the influence of her words. In fact, I inherited that potty mouth honestly.

Now that I'm a mom, I've felt the burden of wondering if I'm totally and completely screwing up my kids. Sometimes I feel like I'm just closing my eyes and hoping the good things will stick and the bad things will be forgotten. It's this mind-set that can leave me with crushing disappointment the moment my child starts developing a fear I know she saw first in me or the moment she turns to a heap of sugary goodness or screens to find comfort, the way I do sometimes.

Here's what I want you to know though: the language of my mom's prayers sank deeper into my soul than those four-letter words did. As we strive to be perfect mommas, with all the best of intentions, we have to remember we will never be perfect. And thank goodness, God never asked us to be. Here's what he did ask us to do: "Love the LORD your God with all your heart and with all your soul and with all your might. And these words that I command you today shall be on your heart. You shall teach them diligently to your children, and shall talk of them when you sit in your house, and when you walk by the way, and when you lie down, and when you rise" (Deuteronomy 6:5-7, ESV).

These verses are a call to teach our kids about the Lord—and to live it out. My momma did that well. When I look back on my childhood, sure, I remember the choice words. But I over-whelmingly remember the prayers and how they impacted my entire life. I learned how to cuss, but I also learned how to pray and ask forgiveness from a loving God who cared enough to hear me confess the four-letter word I voiced in frustration.

There's so much grace in this passage from Deuteronomy. It doesn't call us to be perfect; it instructs us to constantly turn our hearts back to the one who is. Honestly, if our focus is on being perfect, even if we're doing it in the name of Jesus, it pulls the focus away from God and back onto ourselves.

We're going to get some things wrong as moms. We're going to accidentally teach our kids to be fearful or pessimistic or impatient simply by living those things out in front of them. Of course, we hope that we're being transformed by truth and that they will learn amazing things through how we live too, but we can't beat ourselves up for the cracks that will inevitably happen.

When my kids make the same kinds of mistakes I do, I hope they won't strive to fix their mistakes apart from Christ. Instead, I want them to run headlong into the grace of a God they know, because that's what Momma did with her mistakes.

ACTION STEP

Ask yourself the following questions: What am I pouring my energy into when it comes to what I teach my kids? Am I focusing on the things that matter most? Am I teaching them about the Lord, or am I too distracted by my own failures?

PRAYER

Lord, today I come to you with a short and sweet request: let my mistakes point my kids to you. In Jesus' name, amen.

MORNING QUESTIONS

TAKEAWAY TODAY | *What good things did you learn from your mom? What bad habits did you learn from her?*

What spiritual legacy are you leaving for your kids?

DREADING TODAY | *Is there anything you're dreading today?*

REDEFINING TODAY | *If so, what is another way you can view that thing you're dreading?*

ASKING GOD TODAY | *What request are you bringing before the Lord today?*

EVENING QUESTIONS

REFLECTION | *In what ways did you and your kids experience God's grace today?*

LITTLE VICTORIES | *Where did you see God show up even in small ways, reminding you that you aren't alone?*

WHITE FLAG MOMENTS | *When did you want to hide or escape today?*

MEMORY OF THE DAY | *What do you want to relish and thank God for?*

MY PRAYER

FEELING UTTERLY ILL-EQUIPPED

HAVE YOU EVER HAD one of those days when you start out proud that you actually remembered to get the Dora the Explorer cards from the dollar store for Valentine's Day—that is, until your child brings home a backpack full of Pinterest-worthy treats? If so, you're in good company. Jesus' disciples had a day when they felt terribly ill-equipped for the task ahead of them, too.

Here's what happened. Thousands of people had just spent the day listening to Jesus, but it was going to get dark soon and there was no food anywhere nearby. The disciples assessed the situation and told Jesus to send the people away to grab some food. As a girl who doesn't skip a meal, I would have been grateful for a disciple who watched the clock, kept the preaching on track, and cared about the people's appetites.

But then Jesus, in all his Jesus-ness, took the disciples far outside the box when he casually told them to give the people something to eat. In Matthew 14:16 Jesus says, "They do not need to go away. You give them something to eat" (NIV).

As if they had a food truck fully stocked just beyond the hill!

They answered about the way you'd imagine. "Um . . . we only have, like, two fish and five loaves of bread." But you know how the story goes. Jesus literally turned what they did have into more than enough.

On any given day, I feel the same way. Ill-equipped. Like I have two fish and five loaves of bread, and I need to feed a small army. Like God just asked me to do something that seems impossible.

But here was the mistake of the disciples—and the mistake I make too. We picture these moments without God.

What's crazy is that Jesus had already been performing miracles that day, healing lots of people. The disciples knew what he was capable of, but in that moment they did the math of adding two fish and five loaves and forgot to multiply it by what God could do with it.

If God is asking you to do something, he's going to equip you. That might not mean it will be easy, but he's going to give you what you need.

Where it gets tricky is when we stop looking to him for the *how*.

How is God equipping you to make it through this rough day? The answer will look different for each person—for each day, even. But he *will* provide.

What seems like a small lunch of fish and bread is more than enough—as long as God is involved. I would wager that the moments of equipment failure happen when we are trying to do things on our own. It's the days I know I serve a God of impossible things that have a completely different tone.

Back to those disciples. What if they'd said, "Okay, Jesus. We'll head out and look for food" and about-faced, heading for the nearest town to figure it out on their own? Personally, I'd be shaking my head in judgment. *You have no money, and you're*

trying to get food for five thousand–plus people on your own?
When Jesus is right here? Disciples, come on! Then again, how
often have we received a word from God and then about-faced
to figure out the how on our own? Or what if the disciples had
said, "Can't be us, Jesus. We have nothing to offer"? Would they
have expected Jesus to say, "Oh, I must have gotten the wrong
guys. My bad"? How often do we toss our hands in the air and
tell God he has the wrong girl?

Can we keep that picture with us as we think about our own
lives? Maybe you only got four hours of sleep last night. It's not
much, but that plus Jesus will get you through this day. Not four
hours plus an about-face to the coffee machine. Not four hours
plus an about-face to your phone.

Mommas, today let's trust that if God has asked us to do
something, he'll do it through us. We just have to be willing to
ask him how.

ACTION STEP

List all the things you feel ill-equipped to handle. Then
ask God *how*—how he is equipping you to do this today.

PRAYER

Father, I don't have the answers. Forgive me for
the times I subconsciously believe I do. It never
ends well. Turn my two fish and five loaves into
more than enough. I trust that you have the
answers and will equip me for what you have
already asked me to do. In Jesus' name, amen.

MORNING QUESTIONS

TAKEAWAY TODAY | *What are your fish and loaves—the small things you have to bring to God?*

What crutches are you most tempted to rely on to get through the day instead of trusting God?

DREADING TODAY | *Is there anything you're dreading today?*

REDEFINING TODAY | *If so, what is another way you can view that thing you're dreading?*

ASKING GOD TODAY | *What request are you bringing before the Lord today?*

EVENING QUESTIONS

REFLECTION | *How did God multiply your little into something big today?*

LITTLE VICTORIES | *Where did you see God show up even in small ways, reminding you that you aren't alone?*

WHITE FLAG MOMENTS | *When did you want to hide or escape today?*

MEMORY OF THE DAY | *What do you want to relish and thank God for?*

MY PRAYER

SLOW AND STEADY
WINS THE RACE

THIS IS SLOW AND STEADY WORK, this parenting thing. There's no Pinterest post for "How to Train Up Your Child in Three Days" or "Five Simple Steps to Spiritual Maturity." It doesn't happen in a flash of light or during a week at summer camp. Training up a child is a daily process, and there's no shortcut.

I think we inherently know that, but my moments of deepest frustration as a mom almost always circle back to a misbehaving child. I can handle a broken dishwasher in isolation. I can handle hot, humid days of running errands with happy kids. But if you throw a whining child into the mix, it's all over. Momma's gonna blow.

I know I'm not alone in this. As I've talked to other moms, I've found that our inner grumpy mom is most often drawn out when we're dealing with misbehaving kids. It's the last straw, the breaking point on our worst days.

You might be hoping that I'll offer you a quick fix for our kids, but unfortunately, I can't do that. I can, however, offer you a new mind-set—one that has helped me handle my moments of weakness with more strength and grace. There's a verse in Proverbs that we usually apply to work and money—but then again, parenting *is* real work (and all the mommas said amen). So I think this truth makes sense in the context of motherhood, too. "Committed and persistent work pays off; get-rich-quick schemes are ripoffs" (Proverbs 28:20, MSG).

As I train up my girls and face everyday struggles myself, I want to cling to the truth of this verse. It helps to remember that training my kids takes committed and persistent work and that a dramatic child should be an expected part of the process, not something that sends me over the edge.

My anger in those moments speaks so much of my demand for a get-mature-quick scheme. Not only is that impossible, but it doesn't pay off. The committed and persistent work is what pays off.

How many moments of yelling and feeling completely over-whelmed could I save myself if I approached my role as a parent with a slow and steady pace instead of setting expectations that my children were never meant to meet? What if, when my daughter loses her mind in the grocery store while my hands are full, I could remember that this is a training ground? That it's a teachable moment for her—and for me, too? In that situation I have two choices: I can completely lose my mind and join her on the floor, or I can remember the process she's going through and speak calmly to her without expecting perfection.

Another version puts Proverbs 28:20 this way: "A faithful person will be richly blessed, but one eager to get rich will not go unpunished" (NIV). I don't want to live overeager for my child's maturity or idolize the end goal so much that I take my eyes off the Lord and what he's doing right now.

As you battle the everyday frustrations of life today, your

kids will no doubt have their biggest breakdowns right in the middle of difficult situations and make them even crazier. That's why it's important to remember, before that even happens, what this process of training is all about. Be committed and persistent, and know that training up a child doesn't stop during the crazy moments of life.

And in those moments when you see fruit, I want you to revel in the progress. Not the fruit of a "fixed" child but the fruit of a calm response. Stay faithful to the slow and steady work, because that's the work God will richly bless.

ACTION STEP

Make note of your slow and steady progress. Write down even the tiniest victories you've experienced lately. Did you speak calmly to your little one who refused to share a toy? Did you avoid harsh or sarcastic words when your teenager didn't clean his or her room the first time you asked?

PRAYER

Father, forgive me for believing there's a rule that demands that my kids show their emotions only if everything else is calm. Give me realistic expectations of them so I don't explode when they melt down in the middle of an already-existing crisis. Give me patience and grace and steadiness to stay committed and persistent. Please bless this slow work! In Jesus' name, amen.

MORNING QUESTIONS

TAKEAWAY TODAY | *When do you find that your inner grumpy mom is most likely to come out?*

In what ways have you seen God at work through the slow and steady process of transformation?

DREADING TODAY | *Is there anything you're dreading today?*

REDEFINING TODAY | *If so, what is another way you can view that thing you're dreading?*

ASKING GOD TODAY | *What request are you bringing before the Lord today?*

EVENING QUESTIONS

REFLECTION | *Were there any situations where you were able to choose persistence today? What happened?*

LITTLE VICTORIES | *Where did you see God show up even in small ways, reminding you that you aren't alone?*

WHITE FLAG MOMENTS | *When did you want to hide or escape today?*

MEMORY OF THE DAY | *What do you want to relish and thank God for?*

MY PRERYER

HE IS WITH ME

GOD HAS SOME PRETTY amazing qualities. And that is the biggest understatement of all time. He's all-powerful, all-knowing, sovereign, holy, majestic, and full of glory. But one simple quality about God that I tend to lose sight of is that he is *with me*.

As we read the story of Joseph in the Old Testament, we notice right away that he didn't have a very easy life. For starters, his brothers were so jealous of him that they sold him into slavery. Then, even after he moved up the ranks in Egypt and it seemed like things were looking up, he was falsely accused and thrown into prison. It looked like he might get a break when the friends he made in prison were released, but they promptly forgot about him after they found freedom. Throughout all those ups and downs, however, one idea is repeated four times: the Lord was with Joseph.

- Genesis 39:2: "The LORD was with Joseph, so he succeeded in everything he did as he served in the home of his Egyptian master."

- Genesis 39:3: "Potiphar . . . realized that the LORD was with Joseph, giving him success in everything he did."
- Genesis 39:21: "The LORD was with Joseph in the prison and showed him his faithful love. And the LORD made Joseph a favorite with the prison warden."
- Genesis 39:23: "The warden had no more worries, because Joseph took care of everything. The LORD was with him and caused everything he did to succeed."

The same is true for us, too. God is with us on that first day we're all alone with a newborn. God is with us when we're wrangling mini grocery-shopping haters into the grocery cart. God is with us when we don't understand why our child is experiencing pain or setbacks.

I don't picture the Lord in prisons. I picture him on the side of green pastures. I picture him at festive Easter egg hunts, inviting the little children into his loving arms. I picture him on the beach. I picture him beckoning us to join him and leave those dank, grubby prisons. I even picture him looking back and beckoning me to hurry up and get to the pastures.

But God wasn't just with Joseph in the good times; he was there every step of the way. And the Lord is right there with us, too, just like he was with Joseph.

Notice that in all four of these verses, some measure of success or favor is mentioned. God is blessing us, even in the midst of what looks and feels hard. His plan is for our good even when things look sketchy.

What should that knowledge do for our confidence? How should our perspective change, knowing we are not alone and we are not forgotten? My hope is that it slows us down and gives us a passion to sense God in our midst. God is not in a rush. We might be, but he's not. And maybe that's why we're so exhausted: we think we have to keep pace with him as we envision him off in the distance in those greener pastures, and we don't realize he's actually right beside us. Isn't it a relief to know we can stop spinning our wheels and just keep pace with the Lord instead of trying to play catch-up?

I want God's presence with me to strengthen my heart and my faith so that each lonely moment is clobbered by this truth: "The Lord is with me."

On those days when I'm short on time and I can't dive into the Word and prayer for an extended period, I want to know that just being in the presence of the Lord brings life and peace to my day.

ACTION STEP

We often live with chronic amnesia of God's presence, when in reality he is right here. Picture Jesus sitting next to you, and hear him say, "I am with you right now." How does that make you feel? How should this affect your life?

PRAYER

Father, bolster me today with the truth that you are with me right now. Show me the power of this truth, and don't let me forget how this changes my life. Let your presence increase my joy and fuel me in a way that only you can do. Free me from the feeling that I'm spinning my wheels, and help me to keep pace with you as I live in your presence. In Jesus' name, amen.

MORNING QUESTIONS

TAKEAWAY TODAY | *When is it easier for you to sense God's presence—in hard times or in good times?*

In what areas of your life do you feel like you're spinning your wheels?

DREADING TODAY | *Is there anything you're dreading today?*

REDEFINING TODAY | *If so, what is another way you can view that thing you're dreading?*

ASKING GOD TODAY | *What request are you bringing before the Lord today?*

EVENING QUESTIONS

REFLECTION | *In what situations did you specifically sense that God was with you today?*

LITTLE VICTORIES | *Where did you see God show up even in small ways, reminding you that you aren't alone?*

WHITE FLAG MOMENTS | *When did you want to hide or escape today?*

MEMORY OF THE DAY | *What do you want to relish and thank God for?*

MY PRAYER

NO PLACE TO GO

I'VE ALWAYS BEEN very driven. Inevitably, every personality test reveals another layer of ambition, drive, a quest for perfection, and attention to detail. This means that I have been able to do a lot of things I set out to do, but it also means I've done it all at a hurried pace. On top of that, it can create a sense of guilt because I know how my personality must exhaust my loved ones (it exhausts me, too!). So many days I have my eyes on the prize, and rarely is it what's right in front of me. The wheels seem to be constantly moving.

I've been on the other end of this too, and in that case there were literal wheels in motion.

I saw an acquaintance in the grocery store and stopped to say hi. I could tell she was in a hurry, and as she kept rolling her cart forward, I felt such pressure to wrap up what I was saying. I felt like an inconvenience.

Is this how my kids feel? Do I rush their souls because they know they have to keep up with my pace if they want my attention? God seems to be hitting this message home in everything I'm reading lately.

First there were Elisabeth Elliot's words: "Often we neglect the thing assigned for the moment because we are preoccupied with something that is not our business just now. How easy it is to give only half our attention to someone who needs us . . . because the other half is focused on a future worry."[2]

Then I came across John Ortberg's book *Soul Keeping*, in which he paints a picture of his mentor, Dallas Willard. His description made this hurried soul slow down: "His face and the movements of his body all seemed to say that he had no place else to go and nothing in particular to worry about."[3] This sounds very simple, but I was mesmerized by the image. There is something comforting about sitting in the presence of someone who has no worries and no place to be.

I want to be a person who puts others at ease because they know that when they are with me, I am all there. I'm not checking my phone repeatedly or watching the clock. I'm not waiting for my turn to talk or to share what I think is brilliant advice.

Instead, I'm able to sit and listen and be present.

I happened to take another personality test recently, and this one highlighted two strengths but also my biggest weakness. It said, "You are not always flexible and can lose sight of others' needs in the pursuit of your goals."

Just in case I hadn't taken Elisabeth's or John's wisdom to heart, this test pegged me to a T. In pursuit of my goals, I tend to lose sight of the needs of everyone around me. I want things that are measurable, and my to-do list is the chief of that. Shepherding my kids' hearts, hearing what my husband is saying between the lines, being there for a friend who's too afraid to ask for help—those things can't be quantified as easily.

If we just can't help but measure things, let's at least change our measuring stick. Hebrews 6:10 says, "God is not unjust; he will not forget your work and the love you have shown him as you have helped his people and continue to help them" (NIV). There may be no immediate item to cross off the list. You may not receive a pat on the back when you listen intently to your littlest one tell the longest story known to humankind or you give your middle schooler yet another ride to practice. But in those moments, can we remember Hebrews 6:10? God sees you. God sees the impact you're making. You are loving on *his* kids each time you choose them over your to-do list. Slow down. Your biggest impact isn't saved for the future. It is right here, right now, with whatever is right before you. Don't let this moment pass you by in hopes of having a greater impact down the road.

ACTION STEP

Meditate on Proverbs 4:25, and keep your eyes straight ahead today.

PRAYER

Father, I need your vision. I am constantly looking to the left and right, behind me, and a thousand steps ahead of me. Show me how to stop calculating and to keep my eyes on what's right in front of me today. Show me how to love those around me with a countenance that says they matter to me and that I have no place else to be. In Jesus' name, amen.

MORNING QUESTIONS

TAKEAWAY TODAY | *Do you know someone who makes you feel like you are their only priority when you're talking to them?*

What would it look like to be fully present in your relationships today?

DREADING TODAY | *Is there anything you're dreading today?*

REDEFINING TODAY | *If so, what is another way you can view that thing you're dreading?*

ASKING GOD TODAY | *What request are you bringing before the Lord today?*

EVENING QUESTIONS

REFLECTION | *Were there any times throughout the day when you prioritized a person over your to-do list?*

LITTLE VICTORIES | *Where did you see God show up even in small ways, reminding you that you aren't alone?*

WHITE FLAG MOMENTS | *When did you want to hide or escape today?*

MEMORY OF THE DAY | *What do you want to relish and thank God for?*

MY PRARYER

Day 11

THE ONE WHO SHALL
REMAIN NAMELESS

MOST DAYS, I assume the devil is in the details—and I mean that literally.

- Bad day? The devil is trying to pull me down.
- Bad Wi-Fi connection? The devil is trying to thwart my work.
- Bad kids? The devil in pigtails.
- Bad shopping experience? The devil in a red polo and khakis.

Okay, just kidding about the last two. But I do give the devil too much power sometimes. I want to recognize that we have an enemy who is looking to steal, kill, and destroy us (John 10:10), but I also don't want to give him too much credit, knowing that as believers, we have the power to resist his temptations (1 Corinthians 10:13).

When I picture the devil, I tend to imagine someone who is strong and can easily overpower me, but I forget that he scurries at the mention of the Lord's name. Ephesians 1:22 says, "He put all things [in every realm] in subjection under Christ's feet, and appointed Him as [supreme and authoritative] head over all things in the church" (AMP).

The devil does have the power to tempt us, but he can't force our response. He can't force us to sin. And in Christ, we have the incredible power to resist him.

As I have been writing this book, I have felt heavy attacks from the devil to the point where I thought I would never write another book again. But I know that's the very thing he would want me to do: succumb to the temptation to give up and let him render me powerless.

The devil wants to leave us so fearful that our only response is to bow out of God's incredible plan for our lives. And because one of our greatest missions is to train our kids well, doesn't it make sense that he would try to trip us up daily in our motherhood? Doesn't it stand to reason that our homes are our most action-packed battlefields? The devil wants that territory more than we can even imagine.

We have to fight hard, knowing that we have the power through Jesus Christ to defeat the evil one. We are not as weak as we feel some days. James 4:7 says, "Submit to [the authority of] God. Resist the devil [stand firm against him] and he will flee from you" (AMP). Hallelujah! We are not under the authority of Satan. The next time he shows up and tempts you to sabotage your own life, remember the truth of this verse.

I love that we have the example of Jesus being tempted by the devil (Matthew 4). What sticks out to me most is that Jesus had spent the previous forty days fasting and praying. He was armed and ready to do battle with the devil. With all three temptations, he responded to Satan using the Word of God.

I want to learn something valuable from Jesus' example.

I don't want to flub a response or cower in shame or play the victim when temptations come. I want to stand on the Word of God and push the devil out.

Lately my husband and I have been teaching our four-year-old, Vivi, about the devil, and that has to be one of the craziest lessons we've taught yet. As Vivi voices her litany of "I can't," we've started talking about how sometimes the devil wants to make her feel like she can't do things. When this happens, we ask her to echo something like this: "Devil, get out of here! You are a liar, and I am not going to believe you." Then we pray to our heavenly Father, who is so much more powerful than Satan. And though it's her battle, I'm left empowered and wanting to crush the snake in my own life too.

The devil is no match for our powerful God. That's why I'm done saying his name as I end today's devotional. Why waste our time on him when we know that the one "who is in you is greater than the one who is in the world" (1 John 4:4, NIV)?

ACTION STEPS

Write down these verses and have them handy when you feel the one who shall remain nameless press in: John 10:10; Romans 8:38-39; James 4:7; 1 John 4:4.

PRAYER

Father God, you are all-powerful. I know this, but some days I give the devil more power than I should. Make me strong and remind me of the authority I have over him because Christ lives in me. In Jesus' name, amen.

MORNING QUESTIONS

TAKEAWAY TODAY | *Do you tend to give Satan too much credit or not enough?*

Can you think of a time when you used God's Word to speak truth to defeat the evil one?

DREADING TODAY | *Is there anything you're dreading today?*

REDEFINING TODAY | *If so, what is another way you can view that thing you're dreading?*

ASKING GOD TODAY | *What request are you bringing before the Lord today?*

EVENING QUESTIONS

REFLECTION | *How did you see Satan at work today? How did you see God at work even more powerfully?*

LITTLE VICTORIES | *Where did you see God show up even in small ways, reminding you that you aren't alone?*

WHITE FLAG MOMENTS | *When did you want to hide or escape today?*

MEMORY OF THE DAY | *What do you want to relish and thank God for?*

MY PRAYER

Day 12

CHECK YOUR SCHEDULE

GRAB YOUR CALENDAR, momma. We're about to surrender today to the Lord. And as scary as that sounds, on those days when I've willingly offered up my perfectly laid-out (and color-coded!) plans, I've experienced more joy than I've ever found on the pages of a detailed schedule.

But there's a significant difference between surrendering our schedules and chucking them out the window completely. As moms, we are called to create order and structure for our families. We keep track of tests and baseball schedules and play-dates. And I firmly believe in getting things out of our heads and onto paper, because the mind of a momma isn't the most trust-worthy holder of important details! In other words, this totally type-A girl who loves structure doesn't have to hyperventilate at the thought of waking up to an entirely blank page, just waiting for God to fill it up.

Proverbs 16:3 helps me manage this tension: "Commit to the LORD whatever you do, and he will establish your plans" (NIV).

If we are inviting God into the process of how we plan our days, we don't have to fear that God will come in and dismantle the whole thing (or if he does, it will be the exception).

So what does it look like to commit whatever we do to the Lord and put him in charge? Here are a few things I think will help us walk this out, on a practical level:

Big picture. If you make goals at the beginning of the year (or a three- or five-year vision for your family), make sure part of your process is to explicitly ask the Lord what he is calling you to do next. Give him space to respond before you write down a bunch of your own plans. Then hold that list out to him and ask him if there is anything included that shouldn't be there and if there is anything not on the list that should be there.

Seasonal. Pause before saying yes to a new commitment. It's the same principle that applies in marriage: you show respect to your spouse by discussing big decisions with him instead of making the choice on your own. In the same way, we honor God by talking over a decision with him first. This might involve a ten-second pause or a delay of a few days, but get in the habit of leaving some wait time before you commit to something. When we answer immediately, we are voicing our own desires (or trying to please someone else) instead of seeking God's input first.

Daily. We can get just as excited for the unknowns of our day as we can for what we have written down. Psalm 27:14 says, "Wait for and confidently expect the Lord; be strong and let your heart take courage; yes, wait for and confidently expect the Lord" (AMP). That right there is the spice of life—and the remedy for the mom who is overwhelmed with how mundane the tasks of motherhood can be. If your list consists of doing laundry and going grocery shopping, hold that calendar up to the Lord and let him surprise you with what he will bring your way when you surrender it to him!

The Message and the Amplified Bible give us an even clearer picture of Proverbs 16:3. "Put GOD in charge of your work" (MSG) and "your plans will succeed [if you respond to His will and guidance]" (AMP). To respond to God's will and his guidance, we have to seek him consistently in his Word and through prayer and wise counsel. As we do this, we will grow more comfortable on those days when our schedules are completely dismantled, because we trust the God we've grown to know and love.

How exciting to picture a mom who is learning how to surrender her calendar each morning. As she does, this very act of surrender becomes something that brings joy and expectation instead of fear and anxiety.

ACTION STEP

Grab your planner, hold it out, and offer it up to the Lord today.

PRAYER

Father, I long so much to have my plans align with yours. That means giving you the big things as well as the daily things. This morning, I check my schedule and ask you to reevaluate what I have written. If anything doesn't line up with your plan, I give it to you. I choose to obey. In Jesus' name, amen.

MORNING QUESTIONS

TAKEAWAY TODAY | *Are you a planner, or do you tend to just react?*

What part of your schedule is hardest to surrender to the Lord?

DREADING TODAY | *Is there anything you're dreading today?*

REDEFINING TODAY | *If so, what is another way you can view that thing you're dreading?*

ASKING GOD TODAY | *What request are you bringing before the Lord today?*

EVENING QUESTIONS

REFLECTION | *What surprises came your way today as a result of trusting the Lord with your time?*

LITTLE VICTORIES | *Where did you see God show up even in small ways, reminding you that you aren't alone?*

WHITE FLAG MOMENTS | *When did you want to hide or escape today?*

MEMORY OF THE DAY | *What do you want to relish and thank God for?*

MY PRAYER

Day 13

BREATH FOR THE DAY

As you get ready for the day ahead, you might already be exhausted thinking about all the things you need to accomplish. I want to give you some hope today—literally from the mouth of God.

Genesis 2:7 says, "The Lord God formed a man from the dust of the ground and breathed into his nostrils the breath of life, and the man became a living being" (NIV). Did you catch that? God's own breath filled the body of a human being. I tend to dwell on the truth that we were born sinners and that when we become Christians, we invite the Holy Spirit to indwell us. Sometimes I have trouble getting my mind around the fact that there's a supernatural force at work inside me. It's true that the Holy Spirit comes in when we invite him into our hearts, but this account of Creation reminds us that God breathed life into people from the very beginning.

This truth brings comfort and strength to my physically weary bones. I feel like I stand a little taller knowing that I'm

God-breathed. God didn't just throw some sticks together to form man and woman. Sure, dirt and a rib were involved, but this creation wasn't a living being until God breathed life into it. How energizing is that!

As you struggle with a body that's weary from weathering pregnancies, a bad back from carrying babies, dry eyes from a lack of sleep, or tired knees from cleaning the floor, remember this: our human bodies began with the breath of God himself.

Just a few verses before the account of God breathing life into the first human, we read, "God created mankind in his own image, in the image of God he created them; male and female he created them" (Genesis 1:27, NIV). How can this fuel our bodies today? There are so many moments when we feel exhausted, but I believe there are even more moments—literally each new breath—when we can be refueled by the Lord. He offers us moment-by-moment strength.

I have a morning exercise that I like to do (although I don't do it often enough). It's a way to remember that I am not operating out of my own strength but out of the strength of Christ, who lives in me and has filled my lungs with breath. I lie flat on my back on the floor and picture Christ in my heart. Then I stretch out my limbs and visualize him flowing through every part of me. As I reach my fingertips, I picture his strength as I set out for the day. He's in every step and every act of service I do with my hands.

In John Maxwell's book *No Limits,* he talks about pushing past what we think are our limits. He shares this quote by a Navy SEAL: "When you think you're done, you're only at forty percent of what your body is capable of doing. That's just the limit that we put on ourselves." Maxwell asks, "What would happen if you assumed that you had at least 60 percent more capacity than you ever believed? . . . What if it's not 60 percent?

What if it's only 40, or 25, or even 10 percent? Wouldn't that still change your life?"[4] Amen! I'm not banking on the official science of those percentages, but isn't it super freeing to think that we have more capacity in reserves, y'all? As finite human beings, we will max out before we know it. But we can move past our perceived limits because of the limitless God whose very breath is in us.

I want to live in this zone of going beyond what I think I can do so that everything in me will be forced to cry out to God.

As you go about your day today, imagine yourself at the 40 percent line instead of being already past 100 percent. Remember that a limitless God is walking with you and is residing inside you.

ACTION STEP

Take three deep breaths. Picture the breath of God filling up your lungs and strengthening your body today, and walk tall in that truth.

PRAYER

Father, breathe your life into me today the way you did when you created the first people. I can't live without you, Lord, and when I feel like I've hit the end of what I can do, let each breath I take remind me of your power alive in me. In Jesus' name, amen.

MORNING QUESTIONS

TAKEAWAY TODAY | *How close do you feel to capacity right now? Do you feel like you're almost maxed out?*

In what areas of your life do you need God's strength most?

DREADING TODAY | *Is there anything you're dreading today?*

REDEFINING TODAY | *If so, what is another way you can view that thing you're dreading?*

ASKING GOD TODAY | *What request are you bringing before the Lord today?*

EVENING QUESTIONS

REFLECTION | *Were there any moments when you sensed God's breath filling you up and giving you energy when you needed it?*

LITTLE VICTORIES | *Where did you see God show up even in small ways, reminding you that you aren't alone?*

WHITE FLAG MOMENTS | *When did you want to hide or escape today?*

MEMORY OF THE DAY | *What do you want to relish and thank God for?*

MY PRAYER

WHEN QUIET IS SCARY

Raise your hand if you're a momma who would love a little peace and quiet. I think this is the anthem for any mom with a car full of little voices or a house full of busy teenagers.

When I was growing up, my mom always wanted my siblings and me to turn down the music and TV. Me? I loved the background sounds and couldn't understand why she liked the quiet so much. Now that I'm a mom, though, I get it. She was weary from the constant noise. All day long, I get asked questions or hear shrieks every time a toy exchange doesn't go as planned. The quiet is something we mommas come to crave.

As much as I long for those quiet moments, however, it can be pretty scary when they come. And that's not because the silence means my kids are destroying some piece of furniture. That would honestly be easier to clean up. The scary part is where my thoughts go when they finally have a chance to run free.

A few nights ago I had one of these moments. I was so excited to finally have some downtime, and then it started. The fear sank in first. The dread came next. And then the guilt. Oh, the guilt.

When we have a little space to think, we sometimes have trouble taking our thoughts captive, and those blessed moments of silence can end up being draining instead of refreshing—and all the more so because we had such high hopes for how this quiet time would rejuvenate us.

God's Word calls us to "destroy arguments and every lofty opinion raised against the knowledge of God, and take every thought captive to obey Christ" (2 Corinthians 10:5, ESV). When I recognize that this challenge isn't just something I do to feel better but something I do out of obedience to Christ, I take it more seriously.

We have to get deliberate about our thoughts. When we finally get the quiet we long for, we should be able to look forward to it and not subconsciously feel nervous about what will surface.

Life coach Brooke Castillo maps out how our thoughts work and gives us a practical way to change them. Though her approach is not necessarily biblically based, it falls in line with 2 Corinthians 10:5, emphasizing how our thoughts determine so much about our actions. This tool has helped me in my journey toward taking my thoughts captive.

> **Circumstances** are things that happen that you can't control.
> **Thoughts** are opinions about your circumstances (this is where we have the power to change things).
> **Feelings** are one-word descriptions of your emotions, which are caused by thoughts, not circumstances.
> **Actions** are anything you do in response to that feeling.
> **Results** are what happen as an effect of actions.[5]

Here's an example based on my normal thought process and where it leads, and then the pattern that happens when I intentionally choose my thoughts.

Natural thought process: free time at night after girls go to sleep→I'm a morning person, and the nights make me feel heaviness and dread→anxious→feeling restless; having trouble falling asleep→unrest.

Changed thought process: free time at night after girls go to sleep→there is a creative energy that happens when the sun is down and the house is quiet→invigorated and expectant→reading books and writing ideas; falling asleep more peacefully without regret or guilt→refreshment.

We have to protect our thoughts and choose them intentionally. I want refreshment for you and for me. When we finally get space to think and breathe, I don't want our thoughts to run roughshod over us and take us somewhere we don't want to go. The stronger our muscles are for taking our thoughts captive, the more joyful every quiet moment will be—and the loud ones too.

ACTION STEP

Think of a recent circumstance that spiraled into negative thoughts, and then write the series of events based on this model. Then write out what this could look like if the negative thoughts were taken captive.

PRAYER

Father God, give me wisdom to take my unruly thoughts captive and make them obedient to you. I long to obey you in all areas of my life, but somehow I forget that this applies to my thoughts, too. I'm expectant to see how you change my thoughts and, in turn, change my life. In Jesus' name, amen.

MORNING QUESTIONS

TAKEAWAY TODAY | *When is it hardest for you to take your thoughts captive?*

Why do you think God cares so much about our thoughts?

DREADING TODAY | *Is there anything you're dreading today?*

REDEFINING TODAY | *If so, what is another way you can view that thing you're dreading?*

ASKING GOD TODAY | *What request are you bringing before the Lord today?*

EVENING QUESTIONS

REFLECTION | *What thoughts were you able to successfully take captive today? What thoughts spiraled out of control today?*

LITTLE VICTORIES | *Where did you see God show up even in small ways, reminding you that you aren't alone?*

WHITE FLAG MOMENTS | *When did you want to hide or escape today?*

MEMORY OF THE DAY | *What do you want to relish and thank God for?*

MY PRAYER

MY PRAYER

YOUR GO-TO EXCUSE

EXCUSES. WE ALL HAVE THEM. We all have a reason for our grumpy faces or for why we just aren't ourselves some days.

I'll go first. Lately my excuse for not having regular, reliable joy is because I feel like the whole universe is out to get me. I realize that sounds quite melodramatic. But seriously, every major deadline or project I've had in the past two months has been preceded by a big sickness for one of my kids. Most recently, my two girls volleyed a fever back and forth all week, dropped it for a few days, and then picked it right up again.

I always manage to convince myself that my excuses are good enough to steal my joy. I believe that they have a right to my joy more than I do. I believe that I can have joy as soon as these pesky things stop happening to me and leave me alone to my joy. This line of reasoning is completely false, but it's something I seem to believe, judging from how I let anything run away with my joy.

What's your excuse for not having joy? What is the most common culprit for your momma malaise?

It's time for some tough love for all of us: whatever our excuse, it's not good enough.

I'm not saying this because life is easy. I won't pretend to understand the dark days for the mom who loses a child or walks through cancer with a spouse. But more often than not, at least for me, the situations that snag my joy aren't the big things; they're the low-level pains and frustrations. It's almost like we *want* our excuses to be good enough—we are trying to prove to the world, "See, I told you! I should be allowed to be miserable, and now that I've told you all the details, don't you agree?" As crazy as it sounds, we are becoming a generation of mommas who are looking for a way out of having joy. We try to outdo each other in who has motherhood the hardest.

In John 5, Jesus and the disciples arrive at a healing pool, a place where those who couldn't walk came looking to be healed. When Jesus gets there, he asks a lame man, "Do you want to get well?"

This seems like an odd question at first. But I've been in a similar spot myself. *Yes, but . . .*

Yes, but nobody can help me.
Yes, but I've been sitting here for so long.
Yes, but I don't know if it will ever happen.

Do we roll our eyes at this man's excuse when Jesus is about to offer healing? Then again, if God asked us, "Do you want joy?" would we have any "Yes, but" responses?

Yes, but I have all these bad circumstances.
Yes, but have you seen my kids lately?
Yes, but nothing ever seems to work out for me the way it
    does for my Facebook friend Ms. Overly Peppy Poppy.

Maybe Jesus wasn't asking if the man wanted to get well as much as he was asking if the man would *choose* to be healed. Just like healing for this man, joy is a choice, and we've been opting out for too long.

Throughout the day, we have bidders for our joy. From the low bidders, like locking our keys in the car, to high bidders, like totaling the car, we are constantly tempted to sell our joy. Let's commit to a perspective shift. Keys locked in the car will not get me down. A chaotic trip to the grocery store will not steal my joy.

Today is our chance. Today is our choice. We get to choose to "get well." Our joy is not for sale. And if I can take this metaphor even further? If it were for sale, it wouldn't matter, because it has already been paid for by the highest of bidders: Jesus at the Cross. Going, going, gone.

ACTION STEP

Change the conversation with another mom today. Share what tried to steal your joy and the victory you experienced from refusing the bid. Or if something bid and you took the offer, confess that and allow it to be a moment you can both learn from. Just be careful not to let it end in an impromptu pity party!

PRAYER

Father, my joy has been up for grabs every day, and the bidders are many. Help me to hold on to my joy, knowing you paid the price to save me. Please allow me to experience the fullness of your joy. In Jesus' name, amen.

MORNING QUESTIONS

TAKEAWAY TODAY | *What is your go-to excuse for not having joy?*

What reasons do you have for embracing joy today?

DREADING TODAY | *Is there anything you're dreading today?*

REDEFINING TODAY | *If so, what is another way you can view that thing you're dreading?*

ASKING GOD TODAY | *What request are you bringing before the Lord today?*

EVENING QUESTIONS

REFLECTION | *Were there any moments today when something tried to steal your joy? How did you respond?*

LITTLE VICTORIES | *Where did you see God show up even in small ways, reminding you that you aren't alone?*

WHITE FLAG MOMENTS | *When did you want to hide or escape today?*

MEMORY OF THE DAY | *What do you want to relish and thank God for?*

MY PRAYER

BREAK THE CYCLE

I GET MYSELF INTO the craziest of pickles. Well, that's the nice way to put it. It's more like a downward spiral that never seems to hit bottom.

Over the last few weeks, I've been sprinting into dumb decisions—ones I know are not the way to abundance in my life. Yet I keep choosing them. For me it looks like this: I stay up way too late reading about the latest royal gossip or Hollywood breakup (I can't believe I just admitted that). I regret going to bed late, and I end up waking up late and missing quiet time with the Lord. I feel sluggish and too tired to take my vitamins and eat good food, making me feel even more sluggish, so I sit the girls in front of the TV and plop myself on the couch instead of engaging their minds or prepping dinner. By late afternoon, we have a messy house, grouchy kids, an exhausted mom, and no dinner in sight. This pushes back bedtime again, leaving less than adequate time to get ready for the next day or to spend quality time with the man I love. I end the night guilt ridden, bemoaning my bad choices and drowning my sorrows in social media, only to go to bed late and repeat the cycle all over again.

It kills me that I keep doing this, because I know better. But it's a hard cycle to break. Not today, though. It was only by the skin of my teeth, but I did it. Nap time rolled around, and although I had plenty of work to do and my littlest was refusing to lie down in her crib, I picked up that Bible that's been collecting dust all week and I chose the good.

What's crazy is that I almost convinced myself to take care of the laundry instead of meet with my heavenly Father. I spent half an episode of a comedy show folding towels. Now, there's nothing inherently wrong with watching a show (or folding laundry, for that matter). In that moment, though, I knew I was dodging God and choosing everything but him.

My exit ramp from the cycle was to spend time with the Lord to realign my thoughts to his truth. I needed to stop the narrative that my life was really hard and that I wasn't capable of handling it all. I needed to stop defining myself with words that should never define someone who is wrapped in the righteousness of Christ.

It was the smallest of choices, but it shifted everything and generated even more good choices. As I read the Word, this verse caught my attention: "Turn my eyes from worthless things, and give me life through your word" (Psalm 119:37). That's pretty direct, isn't it? Sometimes I need it straight. And sometimes I need to literally turn my eyes from worthless things and go to the Word.

Vana is in a phase where she has a hard time holding still long enough to hear what I'm saying. Many days I have to hold her chubby little cheeks in my hands until I have her attention. Inevitably, though, her eyes dart to the side, and I'm sitting there thinking how silly she is to work sooooo hard to look away from me when I'm in her line of vision. I wonder how silly God thinks I am when I keep my eyes on the royal wedding instead of on the truth in his Word that reminds me I'm the daughter of the King.

It's time for us to commit right now to taking the first exit ramp out of those cycles that distance us from God's best for our lives—and ultimately from God himself. The good news is that there are opportunities throughout the day to break the cycle of whatever is keeping us in a pattern of bad choices. Let's rejoice in the fact that we aren't bound to remain in our downward spiral—God has lined the path of distraction with exit ramps.

ACTION STEP

Meditate on Psalm 119:10 (the Amplified version is my favorite for this passage), and break the cycle right here, right now. Make one small choice that will break whatever funk you are in.

PRAYER

Father, turn my eyes from worthless things and give me life through your Word. Give me an alertness to the next exit ramp and help me to walk in obedience to take it. In Jesus' name, amen.

MORNING QUESTIONS

TAKEAWAY TODAY | *What does your typical downward spiral look like?*

Can you think of a time when God met you in his Word and broke the cycle you were stuck in?

DREADING TODAY | *Is there anything you're dreading today?*

REDEFINING TODAY | *If so, what is another way you can view that thing you're dreading?*

ASKING GOD TODAY | *What request are you bringing before the Lord today?*

EVENING QUESTIONS

REFLECTION | *What exit ramps did the Lord provide for you today? How did you respond?*

LITTLE VICTORIES | *Where did you see God show up even in small ways, reminding you that you aren't alone?*

WHITE FLAG MOMENTS | *When did you want to hide or escape today?*

MEMORY OF THE DAY | *What do you want to relish and thank God for?*

MY PRAYER

GOING OFF THE CLOCK

THE MOST PHILOSOPHICAL of lessons today: we need to learn to live a little.

I mean, I hope we live a lot, but let's start with living a little.

If you are anything like me, the list of things that must get done keeps you in a constant cycle of productivity. We don't know the definition of a joyride, and we can't fathom watching Netflix without laundry, meal planning, or a project in hand. And on the off chance that today has zero worries (a miracle in itself), we go borrowing some from tomorrow and the next day. We're proactive like that. On days when we feel like we're finally caught up, we don't take it as a sign to relax and enjoy life but as a time to get ahead and prepare for the next bump.

Is it any wonder we can feel so weary? When we finally catch a break, we don't take it! Or is it just me?

Paul reminds us that enjoying the easy days is something we likely need to learn. Philippians 4:12-13 says, "I know how to get along and live humbly [in difficult times], and I also know how to enjoy abundance and live in prosperity. In any and every circumstance I have learned the secret [of facing life], whether well-fed or going hungry, whether having an abundance or being in need" (AMP).

If enjoying abundance were easy, Paul wouldn't have needed to include it in the list of things he'd learned. Of course it's impressive that he figured out how to live with little. We know how difficult that is. But he made sure to mention that he'd learned the secret to living in abundance, too. If Paul had to learn this lesson, I'm taking that as a sign that we don't need to beat ourselves up over the fact that we haven't mastered it yet.

I, for one, am still a novice at this. I am married to a "fun guy." I can't tell you the number of times he has suggested that we do something fun—something that added no value to my to-do list and that I saw as a complete waste of time! There have been times when I've even gotten frustrated that he would suggest such a thing when our to-do list wasn't complete. The nerve!

How about you? Does your mind tend to drift to tackling the next item on your to-do list instead of enjoying the moment? If so, we're going to learn together how to embrace the good days and, like Paul says, to enjoy the abundance and live in prosperity.

The first step in learning to enjoy the moment is to recognize our love for numbers. Yes, even a word lover like me loves the numbers. I want everything to be measurable, and if it isn't, I don't think it's worth my time. This is faulty thinking. Pastor and author Peter Scazzero says, "The Sabbath calls us to build the doing of nothing into our schedules each week. Nothing measurable is accomplished."[6]

When I read this, I breathed a heavy sigh of relief, longing for a weekly day of rest. But guess what? God calls us to unmeasurable moments every day, too.

Let's get really practical here and invoke the "unmeasurable moments" rule. This is a time set aside when we go "off the clock" in the business of being productive. The idea is that eventually we will learn to instinctively inject these moments into every day, but until that happens, we need to find specific triggers to remind us to do this so it actually happens.

ACTION STEP

Set aside a designated time in your day to go off the clock. For me, this is the last hour before bed. If you always have to be doing something, here are some examples of unmeasurable things you can do (but resist the temptation to check them off a list!): linger over Bible reading and prayer; linger over bedtime stories and cuddles; let chats with your spouse last longer—and kissing, too; embrace naps on Sabbath days; read books purely for fun; have a big weekend breakfast; enjoy a French-style dinner with multiple courses that lasts for hours.

PRAYER

Father, teach me to live a little. In my effort to live purposefully, I forget to simply live and I miss out on the joy of each moment. Help me to measure less when you are calling me to rest and enjoy. In Jesus' name, amen.

MORNING QUESTIONS

TAKEAWAY TODAY | *Are you more of a fun-loving person or a productive person? What are the pros and cons to each personality type?*

What "unmeasurable moments" tend to refresh you the most?

DREADING TODAY | *Is there anything you're dreading today?*

REDEFINING TODAY | *If so, what is another way you can view that thing you're dreading?*

ASKING GOD TODAY | *What request are you bringing before the Lord today?*

EVENING QUESTIONS

REFLECTION | *Did you go off the clock today? Were you able to be present in the moment?*

LITTLE VICTORIES | *Where did you see God show up even in small ways, reminding you that you aren't alone?*

WHITE FLAG MOMENTS | *When did you want to hide or escape today?*

MEMORY OF THE DAY | *What do you want to relish and thank God for?*

MY PRAYER

IN SEARCH OF GRATITUDE

I USED TO THINK EXPRESSING GRATITUDE was something we should naturally know how to do. Then, after I had children, I learned it was not.

I will give you exhibit A in my findings: my daughter Vana. As she was learning how to talk, what came out of her mouth was not praise and delight. Instead, her first phrases were demands and complaints—"I want" instead of "I'm grateful for." As Tyler and I have introduced her to the idea of gratitude, I have been recognizing that we are all somewhere on the path of learning gratitude.

I used to think that once I was in the habit of listing a few things I was grateful for each day, I would become a master. But it turns out that I'm still learning. For starters, how do we decide what we should be grateful for? I usually begin with the basics, but on tough days, I tend to stop right after listing a roof over my head and food on my table, as if I can't think of anything else.

I remember one day trying to think of more things to be

thankful for and blanking. Well, not so much blanking as looking around and dwelling on the negatives about each thing my mind landed on. *Grateful for my kids? Yeah, but Vivi's been a monster lately. Grateful for my job? Well, it's really stressful right now, and I'm not making as much money as I'd like to.* I hate to admit it, but this has truly been my thought process some days!

Then John Ortberg goes sticking his nose in my business, saying, "The bigger the sense of entitlement, the smaller the sense of gratitude."[7] Oh, how uncomfortable that makes me! I find it hard to be grateful for things I think I am entitled to. When I take a step back and look at my life without a sense of entitlement, my joy skyrockets and adoration for the Lord wells up inside me.

What would happen if you stopped right now and looked around, realizing that you didn't earn any of what you have? Sure, you may have worked hard to pay for something, but God gave you the job and the skills to work, and God made the place where you live available. All of these are gifts from the Lord.

John Ortberg goes on to give an example of someone going to the dealership to buy a car and someone else who is surprised with a car—topped with a big bow and everything. Who is more grateful? Who enjoys the gift more? The one who felt he earned it, or the one who knew it was a gift?

I love the quote Jennie Allen shares in her book *Anything*: "You have to thank God for the seemingly good and the seemingly bad because really, you don't know the difference."[8] I saw a prime example of this when reading Joseph's speech to his brothers in Genesis 50:20: "You intended to harm me, but God intended it all for good. He brought me to this position so I could save the lives of many people." My simple mind sees Joseph's circumstances (being sold into slavery by his own brothers!) as a major day ruiner, but even something this terrible turned out for good in the end—another reminder that sometimes we don't know what's good and what's bad. So doesn't it make sense to choose to be grateful for all of it instead of hand-selecting what we will thank God for?

This sentiment is highlighted in 1 Thessalonians 5:18 too: "Give thanks in all circumstances; for this is the will of God in Christ Jesus for you" (ESV). God's will for us is a life of gratitude, and that includes no caveats. This is both really scary and really beautiful. Gratitude might feel like a token response—something you learned when you were five—but as we thank the Lord in *all* circumstances, maybe those things that we were complaining about a few days ago are being used by God to sanctify us.

Can we celebrate that victory in the Lord? Just one more thing to be grateful for!

ACTION STEP

Incorporate gratitude into your morning, and begin to recognize those moments when you feel entitled. Discover the joy of trading in entitlement for pure gratitude.

PRAYER

Father, fill my heart with a passion to thank you for everything you've done in my life. Give me eyes of gratitude instead of entitlement, and let that set my joy on fire. Let that gratitude overflow to my entire family, too. In Jesus' name, amen.

MORNING QUESTIONS

TAKEAWAY TODAY | *List three things you're grateful for today.*

What did someone else intend for evil in your life that God is using for good?

DREADING TODAY | *Is there anything you're dreading today?*

REDEFINING TODAY | *If so, what is another way you can view that thing you're dreading?*

ASKING GOD TODAY | *What request are you bringing before the Lord today?*

EVENING QUESTIONS

REFLECTION | *Did you experience any moments of gratitude today—either spontaneous or intentional?*

LITTLE VICTORIES | *Where did you see God show up even in small ways, reminding you that you aren't alone?*

WHITE FLAG MOMENTS | *When did you want to hide or escape today?*

MEMORY OF THE DAY | *What do you want to relish and thank God for?*

MY PRANER

SET THE TEMPERATURE

I THINK WE ALL WANT a home that's filled with more peace and joy and less chaos and tears. If the term *zoo* or *frat house* better defines what happens inside your four walls, today's pep talk is just for you.

But first, a question to consider: Who sets the temperature in your home? Is it you and your spouse? Is it a tug-of-war between the two of you? Do the kids grab chairs and mess with the thermostat?

As you start your day, I want you to believe something that could potentially change your home. *As a momma, you can set the temperature in your home at the start of each day.* You can't decide if a hurricane will blow through, but with a little intentionality, you can set your home and your entire family up for success. Not only that, but you can help everyone get back on track if things get derailed. Because they will.

This is one of the biggest blessings of a joy that isn't determined by circumstances: that same joy seeps out onto other people in your life too. Your decision to choose joy will affect everyone else, and if your outlook is positive, there's a much greater chance theirs will be too.

I'll be honest: I've spent a long time feeling like a victim to my circumstances instead of remembering that as the mom, my mood sets the tone in my home. I see this clearly on my worst days, but I forget that it works in reverse, too. As I'm intentional about our family climate, creating an environment full of giggles and generosity instead of tantrums and taking other people's things, something special starts to take shape. Instead of succumbing to a kid's bad mood and letting it ice over our home, I can warm things up as I recall my own powerful influence.

We are all under the influence of something. Will the biggest influence be the cartoon filled with whiny kids who get their way, or will it be a mom who is patient and full of grace even when things get crazy?

Proverbs 14:1 prompts me to take ownership over the temperature in my home when I would rather choose to believe that what is happening here is out of my control: "The wise woman builds her house [on a foundation of godly precepts, and her household thrives], but the foolish one [who lacks spiritual insight] tears it down with her own hands [by ignoring godly principles]" (AMP). It's not just the storms that blow through that have the power to destroy our homes; our own hands do too. Convicted much?

So what does it look like, practically speaking, to build a foundation on godly precepts? And how do we avoid the other extreme, assuming we can't make a mistake or our home will fold like a house of cards?

This is not a call for perfection. Life is more redeemable than we dare to believe, because even our mistakes can point to Christ. Just the other day I yelled so much that Vivi started covering her ears and acting frightened. I was mortified, and all I could think about was that I had scarred her for life.

As we hopped in the car, I started praying aloud for her school day. Then I confessed my yelling and asked the Lord to forgive me. As we model this kind of repentance, we're teaching a valuable lesson to our children—that our homes don't have to be constantly positive and perfect but that Momma has to go to the source for peace and joy. And that the only way for things to change is for her to go back to God.

The temperature in your home will not stay at a steady seventy-two degrees—it will go up and down depending on circumstances and personalities and emotions. The question is, when crazy weather hits, will you use your influence to bring your home back to a comfortable climate again?

ACTION STEP

Create a morning ritual that reminds you of the influence you have in your home. I like to start the day by diffusing an essential oil called Joy and playing worship music.

PRAYER

Father, let me never take for granted my influence in my home. Help me to shake off any sense of being a victim and instead let me take seriously the call to build my home on godly principles. When things get derailed, show me how I can steer us in a more positive direction, one that ultimately points to you. In Jesus' name, amen.

MORNING QUESTIONS

TAKEAWAY TODAY | *Who or what usually sets the temperature in your house?*

Do you tend to be a thermometer (reflecting the current temperature of your home) or a thermostat (setting the temperature)?

DREADING TODAY | *Is there anything you're dreading today?*

REDEFINING TODAY | *If so, what is another way you can view that thing you're dreading?*

ASKING GOD TODAY | *What request are you bringing before the Lord today?*

EVENING QUESTIONS

REFLECTION | *What did you do today to set the temperature in your home? How effective were you at setting a tone of joy?*

LITTLE VICTORIES | *Where did you see God show up even in small ways, reminding you that you aren't alone?*

WHITE FLAG MOMENTS | *When did you want to hide or escape today?*

MEMORY OF THE DAY | *What do you want to relish and thank God for?*

MY PRAYER

A CHOICE TO MAKE

I LOVE THE STORY of Mary and Martha. And really, I don't know why, because I'm a total Martha. That is highlighted by the fact that I have a twin sister who is a total Mary. I'd be the one tattling on my sister for not working hard enough (and I have been). I'd be the one focused on the task instead of the people (and I have been). In my head, I think I'm doing the tasks for people, which is why I never understood why Jesus didn't seem to appreciate Martha's hard work. She had tidied up and made the food and was waiting on her guests. How could that still not be good enough for Jesus? I think we all know there's a time for both sitting and doing, but what made Mary's decision in this case a better one?

Here's the story from Luke 10:38-42:

> As they were traveling along, [Jesus] entered a village; and
> a woman named Martha welcomed Him into her home.
> She had a sister called Mary, who was seated at the Lord's
> feet, listening to His word. But Martha was distracted
> with all her preparations; and she came up to Him and

said, "Lord, do You not care that my sister has left me to do all the serving alone? Then tell her to help me." But the Lord answered and said to her, "Martha, Martha, you are worried and bothered about so many things; but only one thing is necessary, for Mary has chosen the good part, which shall not be taken away from her" (NASB).

When I read this, the Holy Spirit pressed on me something I hadn't noticed before: *Martha thought she didn't have a choice. Mary knew she did.*

Martha thought the house stuff had to be done. Mary saw it as an option that paled in comparison to sitting at the feet of Jesus.

Martha wasn't going to be able to rest and focus until the chores were done. Mary knew there would always be chores and therefore there's always a choice to make.

The words used to describe Martha are *distracted, worried*, and *bothered*, while the text says that Mary listened intently and chose what was best. The result was a distracted heart for Martha. Mary faced the same possible distractions but chose something different.

Our days are made up of a series of choices. When we wallow in the idea that we have no say in our lives and we must do the laundry and shuttle kids to after-school activities, a lie is planted in our hearts. The result is distraction and frustration with anyone who doesn't seem to work as hard as we do. On top of that, we're still left feeling not good enough.

Have you ever been frustrated with your husband for sitting around while you clean after the kids go to bed? This happened a lot when I was a new mom, and when I talked to Tyler about it, he would say that the mess just didn't bother him the way it did me. He made it seem like it was my choice to clean, which only made me madder. It didn't feel like a choice. It felt like something that had to get done.

But being the limited humans we are, we can't possibly do all the things we think have to get done. So yes, vacuuming is a choice. Boy, I hope it's a choice I make every once in a while at least, but it's a choice nonetheless.

I never want to live distracted from the Father because I'm doing things I feel I have no choice but to do. I don't want to live as if spending time in his presence is something I can't choose daily. I don't want to live with these excuses on the tip of my tongue:

- I can't read my Bible. I have to get the laundry done.
- I can't volunteer for that. I have to make sure I'm home each night to tuck the kids in.
- I can't sit at the feet of Jesus. There are people at the shelter who need another bowl of soup.

We have choices to make. Will we assume we have no choice at all? Or will we realize we have a choice and choose what is essential, like Mary did?

ACTION STEP

Notice all the choices you have to make today. Is there something you can choose not to do today so you can sit at the feet of Jesus?

PRAYER

Father, you know my responsibilities are many, and it's hard for me to figure out what's essential. Help me to sift through the choices and let only what's essential shake out. In Jesus' name, amen.

MORNING QUESTIONS

TAKEAWAY TODAY | *Would you say you are more of a Martha or a Mary?*

What tends to get in the way of you sitting at Jesus' feet?

DREADING TODAY | *Is there anything you're dreading today?*

REDEFINING TODAY | *If so, what is another way you can view that thing you're dreading?*

ASKING GOD TODAY | *What request are you bringing before the Lord today?*

EVENING QUESTIONS

REFLECTION | *Did you have any Mary moments today? What tough choices did you have to make for those moments to happen?*

LITTLE VICTORIES | *Where did you see God show up even in small ways, reminding you that you aren't alone?*

WHITE FLAG MOMENTS | *When did you want to hide or escape today?*

MEMORY OF THE DAY | *What do you want to relish and thank God for?*

MY PRAYER

DARK NIGHT OF
THE BUSY SOUL

I WAS HAVING WHAT I can only describe as a dark night of the soul. My mind was constantly being bombarded with lies, and I couldn't escape them. They were leaving me depressed, hopeless, and exhausted. I wanted to shut off the lies, but I couldn't seem to overcome them.

I had planned to meet some friends downtown for sushi. I knew the twenty-five-minute drive would be too much for my mind to handle alone with my thoughts, so I called my friend Megan. She asked what I needed, and I immediately burst into tears. I needed her to pray. And she did. Megan finished her prayer right as I was pulling up to dinner, and when I found my friends, my face was still tearstained and my eyes were still moist.

That night at dinner, I was all over the place. I felt ashamed when my friends complimented my business and couldn't bring myself to make eye contact. In my head, I analyzed everything I said and the way I was making the rest of the group feel.

My thoughts were volatile and ping-pongy and—dare I say—abusive. On the way home, again afraid to be with my thoughts, I called my mom. Her faith is big, and I needed her to speak some truth over me. And she did.

By the time I reached my doorstep, between Megan's prayer and my mom's dose of truth, something had shifted. There was now a quiet in my soul. Life was still undeniably chaotic, but my soul no longer was. The voices in my head that had been hurling negativity at every turn and keeping me spun up were silenced. I could breathe again.

Have you ever been in a place where you felt that kind of restlessness in your soul? I'm not just talking about busyness here but an internal war zone. My guess is that all of us have been there at some point.

We moms spend a lot of time taking care of everyone around us. We devote untold energy trying to declutter our homes and schedules (which I'm all about), but if we aren't protecting our souls, it won't do us any long-term good.

There's a reason we forget to tend to our souls. It's because our souls whisper when the rest of the world yells. In our hunt to extinguish the loudest dissonant noise, our souls don't even register a blip on the radar. On top of that, soul-tending provides no outward reward. The world sees if I've emptied the dishwasher or passed a test or paid the bills, but it doesn't really notice what's happening in my soul. That means no one can praise me for the work I'm doing there.

I know, this talk of souls may feel a little weird, but the Bible is full of verses about the soul. So I want you to take a deep breath this morning and check the pace of your insides. Matthew 16:26 says, "What will it profit a man if he gains the whole world and forfeits his soul? Or what shall a man give in return for his soul?" (ESV). The value Jesus puts on our souls puts things in perspective for me. Though I might gain the earthly profit of finished chores and public applause, that's a clear loss if I end up forfeiting my soul.

The morning after my dark night of the soul was a revival of sorts. Though the day was anything but leisurely, on the inside I felt like I was deep-breathing on a massage table. It was a good reminder that I can experience peace even if my schedule doesn't slow down. If I allow the Lord to shift the pace of my soul, I can enjoy an unhurried pace no matter how crazy my circumstances get.

There are some things we will simply never be able to change. And if we spend all our energy fighting to change them, we may miss out on the greater benefit of reorienting our souls. I don't necessarily want an immaculately minimalistic life. I just want to feel like my insides are firm and not so squishy. And that, momma, is the official medical term for a soul at rest. Here's to cultivating healthy souls that are "firm and not so squishy."

ACTION STEP

Before you prune a busy schedule, take time to see what your soul needs. Read these verses about the soul: Psalm 42:11; Psalm 62:1; and Jeremiah 6:16.

PRAYER

Father, slow me down—not just my schedule or my physical being, but my soul. Let the steadiness of my insides flow out and bring peace even when circumstances bring chaos. In Jesus' name, amen.

MORNING QUESTIONS

TAKEAWAY TODAY | *Have you ever had a dark night of the soul? What did that experience feel like?*

What would you say your soul needs most right now?

DREADING TODAY | *Is there anything you're dreading today?*

REDEFINING TODAY | *If so, what is another way you can view that thing you're dreading?*

ASKING GOD TODAY | *What request are you bringing before the Lord today?*

EVENING QUESTIONS

REFLECTION | *Were there any moments today when your soul was at rest?*

LITTLE VICTORIES | *Where did you see God show up even in small ways, reminding you that you aren't alone?*

WHITE FLAG MOMENTS | *When did you want to hide or escape today?*

MEMORY OF THE DAY | *What do you want to relish and thank God for?*

—— MY PRAYER ——

Day 22

ON GOOD THINGS

HERE'S AN ODD PHENOMENON I've noticed about the blessings in my life. I've been given so many good things, but for some reason I have trouble enjoying them. You'd think my natural reaction would be to feel grateful and celebrate these gifts, but all too often I end up feeling guilty for the good things—like I can't enjoy them since I don't deserve them.

When we see people suffering in circumstances we can't even fathom, it's natural to want to scrub away the good in our own lives or, at the very least, downplay it. So we tally up reasons why our lives are hard in an attempt to balance the scales somehow. We want to escape the survivor guilt. But this isn't what God intended. Yes, he wants us to empathize with the struggles other people are going through (Romans 12:15), but he also wants us to enjoy the gifts he so generously gives us (Ecclesiastes 3:12-13).

So if life is good right now, ditch the thought that you don't deserve it. That's the world trying to twist God's good gifts into something ugly. No, you don't deserve these good things. But none of us deserve any good thing. James 1:17 says, "Every good and perfect gift is from above, coming down from the Father of the heavenly lights, who does not change like shifting shadows" (NIV). Everything we have is a gift from a mind-blowingly generous God. Instead of rationalizing why it's not that good so we don't feel bad about having it, we can point others to the gift giver by trying something wild: we can stop feeling guilty and, with a grateful heart, just enjoy it.

Momma, why is this so revolutionary? Maybe it seems too laid back while we're over here trying to take life seriously. Or maybe we're so busy analyzing things that enjoying the good days doesn't even occur to us.

If you're anything like me, you feel like you're most "useful" to others when you're going through something challenging. You figure you can illuminate Christ only when you are in the valley. Surely the most enticing and impactful stories are the ones full of trials, right?

You might have friends all around you who are suffering while everything is going pretty well for you at the moment. But feeling guilty won't add anything to their lives. Obviously, we don't want to throw our gifts in their faces, but our complaining in an attempt to even the scales and not come off as "luckier" than they are might actually make things harder for them.

Oh friend, let's allow every good thing in our lives to point to Christ instead of downplaying the gifts and assuming that trials are the only way to glorify him.

If life is good today and you're feeling guilty about it, stop right now and enjoy the gifts God has given you. Don't get bogged down by feeling unworthy. After all, it's that very unworthiness that speaks to God's incredible love for us! When we show gratitude to God for the good things he has given us, he gets all the glory. Our inability to earn these gifts means we can't attribute them to something we did. It's all him!

Most people know of a God who disciplines and judges, but let's fill them in on the gracious character of our God and not hide the good or discount it. Isaiah 30:18 says, "The LORD longs to be gracious to you; therefore he will rise up to show you compassion. For the LORD is a God of justice. Blessed are all who wait for him!" (NIV). I melt when I read this. The Lord *longs* to be gracious to us.

I want my response to every gracious act to be gratitude, not downplaying or discounting what God has done. I want my gratitude to well up celebration and praise inside me. Isn't it gracious of the heavenly Father to offer such good gifts to his kids?

ACTION STEP

Write out the good things in your life right now—including the things that feel almost too easy. Find a way to share your gratitude with others in a way that brings hope and points them to Jesus.

PRAYER

Father, forgive me for questioning the good gifts you've given me. I want so desperately to enjoy them, but my thoughts tell me I don't deserve them and then guilt takes over. Free me from the guilt, and help me to enjoy every good gift that comes from you. In Jesus' name, amen.

MORNING QUESTIONS

TAKEAWAY TODAY | *What are some of the good gifts in your life right now?*

When have you found yourself downplaying or feeling guilty about the good things in your life?

DREADING TODAY | *Is there anything you're dreading today?*

REDEFINING TODAY | *If so, what is another way you can view that thing you're dreading?*

ASKING GOD TODAY | *What request are you bringing before the Lord today?*

EVENING QUESTIONS

REFLECTION | *Were there any moments today when you were able to share your gratitude with someone else?*

LITTLE VICTORIES | *Where did you see God show up even in small ways, reminding you that you aren't alone?*

WHITE FLAG MOMENTS | *When did you want to hide or escape today?*

MEMORY OF THE DAY | *What do you want to relish and thank God for?*

MY PRAYER

BETTER THAN BLAH

WHEN I WAS YOUNGER (okay, a few years ago), I liked to stack the deck for my birthday with every "favorite" I could cram into the day. My favorite outfit, my favorite breakfast, my favorite people, my favorite indulgence, my favorite lunch, my favorite afternoon pastime, my favorite treat from the coffee shop, my favorite dinner. (Food in general was clearly a favorite.)

I had my mind set on the idea that my big day should be full of everything I loved most. I'm not sure where I got this idea, but I don't necessarily recommend it, as this plan failed me miserably. Things never went exactly how I hoped, and based on the way I acted, you would have thought something much more tragic than Starbucks being out of chocolate chip muffins had occurred.

On my birthday each year, I decided that mundane meant miserable. And inevitably, despite my best efforts, the mundane always managed to creep in.

When I talk to other moms, the consensus seems to be that the toughest part of motherhood isn't the really hard stuff but the mundane moments—the days when the most exciting thing to happen is pot roast. Ho hum. That's how we describe most of our days.

I remember feeling this struggle with the ordinary just a few months after my family exited a really difficult season. The truth is, during those really hard days, I would have begged for a little blah. But just a few weeks later, I was unhappy with it.

It's crazy how temptation works and how our flesh bends in those subtle moments to keep us dissatisfied with our lives. We have salvation in our hearts and heaven in view, and here we are, bellyaching about the days running together a bit.

But when I keep the truth of Philippians 2:3-5 in view, I know what I'm doing is anything but ho hum: "Do nothing out of selfish ambition or vain conceit. Rather, in humility value others above yourselves, not looking to your own interests but each of you to the interests of the others. In your relationships with one another, have the same mindset as Christ Jesus" (NIV). The Bible repeatedly calls us to imitate Christ. He humbly served people and sacrificed himself for others. Doesn't it stand to reason that every time we serve our kids, we are glorifying Christ?

I know it feels like we're *just* making lunches and *just* cleaning up spills and *just* changing diapers and *just* hustling to work to pay the bills, but there's more to it than that. I have a feeling you've already heard plenty of people talk about the glory in the mundane, but the reason we're all still talking about it is because every day brings more mundane moments that blur together.

The good news is that there's more to our ordinary moments than we can grasp in our limited perspective. When we see things through the eyes of Christ, the little things take on eternal meaning. When the Israelites were rebuilding the Temple after their exile, God gave the prophet Zechariah a message about how God can use small things for big purposes: "Do not despise these small beginnings, for the LORD rejoices to see the work begin" (Zechariah 4:10).

When I view doing the dishes and laundry apart from a bigger purpose, I want to trade in my dread for an understanding that this is Kingdom work. I want to expect more moments of glory instead of expecting the mundane. That should give us hope, knowing that we don't just have to endure another carpool trip or another evening bath; we can make these moments times of worship.

As you face a day of mundane moments, let this truth hit your soul: the ordinary things that fill your day are just giving you more opportunities to worship the Lord.

ACTION STEP

Write down the moments in your day that seem the most mundane. Create a reminder for those moments that will transform your day. For example, when I'm making the bed, I pray for rest and energy for the day and for great communication between my husband and me. I'm no longer thinking about the drudgery of menial tasks; instead, I'm being reminded that I'm a prayer warrior who is influencing change as I pray.

PRAYER

Father, I give you all the space you need to overcome the seemingly mundane moments of my days and infuse them with your presence. You bring life everywhere you go, and I pray you'd fill this home today. In Jesus' name, amen.

MORNING QUESTIONS

TAKEAWAY TODAY | *What do you find more challenging as a mom: the mundane moments or the big trials?*

What mundane tasks do you find most ho hum?

DREADING TODAY | *Is there anything you're dreading today?*

REDEFINING TODAY | *If so, what is another way you can view that thing you're dreading?*

ASKING GOD TODAY | *What request are you bringing before the Lord today?*

EVENING QUESTIONS

REFLECTION | *Were there any mundane moments that you were able to see as acts of worship today?*

LITTLE VICTORIES | *Where did you see God show up even in small ways, reminding you that you aren't alone?*

WHITE FLAG MOMENTS | *When did you want to hide or escape today?*

MEMORY OF THE DAY | *What do you want to relish and thank God for?*

MY PRAYER

Day 24

IT'S NOT A HUMBLE BRAG

CAN WE TALK ABOUT Christmas for a second? You might be reading this in the heat of summer, but this lesson applies to every season, so I want to share it anyway.

We all talk a big game about not being too busy and not getting overwhelmed at the holidays. We all know we should slow down and enjoy the season instead. But there are so many things out of our control, and life never goes the way we plan. Despite our best efforts, we still end up busy and overwhelmed. Last Christmas, after feeling discouraged that another Christmas was about to go by without any significant slowdown, God hit me with a much-needed reality check:

You are human.
You have finite resources.
You won't do everything on your list.
You won't get the perfect present for everyone.
You won't have twenty-five days of calm and deep meaning.

You may ruin the entire meal you prepare for guests.
You might have the toddler who screams all through the
    Christmas service.

But guess what? If we could control all those things on our
own, we wouldn't need Jesus.
Bam.
Release every bit of guilt you have about being too busy.
Sure, we should try to prioritize our time in a way that reflects
what's in our hearts, but if things don't slow down, may this
overwhelmed feeling remind us of our overwhelming need for
Jesus. Let every moment we feel like we don't measure up or
can't do it on our own remind us that this is actually the reason
Jesus came. He came to save us because we couldn't save ourselves. Luke 19:10 says, "The Son of Man came to seek and to
save the lost" (NIV). Jesus didn't come to watch us be perfect.
He didn't come to cheer us on or even encourage us. He came to
save us. If you feel like you are drowning, that's the gospel coming to life. Grab hold of it. May every moment of weakness in
your day be a chance to revel in the grace of a merciful God.

Paul describes his thorn in the flesh this way: "Each time
[the Lord] said, 'My grace is all you need. My power works
best in weakness.' So now I am glad to boast about my weaknesses, so that the power of Christ can work through me"
(2 Corinthians 12:9). I love that Paul boasts about his weakness. At first I thought this sounded a little showy of him, like
he was trying to outdo every other believer. He's not just okay
with his weaknesses, but he's actually boasting about them?
Seriously, Paul?

On my really rough days, though, I start to piece together
where Paul is coming from. It's not a humble brag. He knows full
well that no matter how hard he tries, he will never come close

to achieving the power of Christ at work in him. That means that if Christ's power shows up when he's weak and surrendered, he's going to be stronger than if he had relied on his own ability.

Momma, I have no idea what's going to come your way today, but I do know this: if we start treating every weak moment the way Paul did instead of letting it riddle us with guilt, our days will radically change. We don't have to be afraid of not measuring up. We don't have to let guilt consume us and distract us from our kids. We don't have to feel insecure with our spouses. And for goodness' sake, we can stop believing the lie that someone could parent our kids better than we could. God picked you. He came to save you. He doesn't want perfection from you; he wants you to be made perfect in your weakness.

So rest, momma. You aren't starting this day behind the curve. You are right where you need to be. And he's right there with you.

ACTION STEP

Write down three of your biggest hang-ups or things you feel guilty over. Ask God to fill up that weakness and make you stronger than you ever imagined.

PRAYER

Father, thank you for each of my weaknesses. Give me the power to resist the temptation to feel guilty about them. Instead, may I boast in my weakness and invite your power to work in me. I know the outcome will be better than anything I could come up with in my own strength. In Jesus' name, amen.

MORNING QUESTIONS

TAKEAWAY TODAY | *When do you tend to feel most overwhelmed?*

How does it feel to know that Paul struggled with his weaknesses too?

DREADING TODAY | *Is there anything you're dreading today?*

REDEFINING TODAY | *If so, what is another way you can view that thing you're dreading?*

ASKING GOD TODAY | *What request are you bringing before the Lord today?*

EVENING QUESTIONS

REFLECTION | *In what ways did you sense God refining you through your weaknesses today?*

LITTLE VICTORIES | *Where did you see God show up even in small ways, reminding you that you aren't alone?*

WHITE FLAG MOMENTS | *When did you want to hide or escape today?*

MEMORY OF THE DAY | *What do you want to relish and thank God for?*

MY PRAYER

THE ART OF REDIRECTION

I LEARNED THE GREAT ART of redirection from parenting my kids. Sometimes in an effort to not completely squash their spirits, I redirect them instead of teaching them their thousandth lesson of the day. Instead of going into another drawn-out explanation about the foolish choice they are about to make, I simply turn their attention elsewhere and give us both a break from the unending "teachable moments."

The simple redirect shifts us from a path of potential destruction and gives us a small victory that my kid can remember too. "Vivi, you didn't throw a fit about having to wear those shoes! Bravo!" We can go about our day in a new direction without having to pound out the result.

Momma, I want that for you and me too. When we are tempted to worry, get frustrated with our kids or spouse, or feel lost in what's next, we have the opportunity to redirect those thoughts and turn them into prayers. This will allow us to walk forward in victory.

Anxieties, annoyances, and unknowns can distract us from

our great mission of shepherding our kids. The ability to turn these moments over quickly and set them on a new path is truly a gift from God—and a super practical one. So let's talk about three types of negative, distracting thoughts that we can redirect.

WORRIES INTO PRAYERS

When worries creep in, let's not try to hide those thoughts from the Lord because we feel like we should handle them on our own or because we are ashamed of our worry. Nope, let's hand our worries straight to him. The Message paraphrases Philippians 4:6-7 this way: "Don't fret or worry. Instead of worrying, pray. Let petitions and praises shape your worries into prayers, letting God know your concerns. Before you know it, a sense of God's wholeness, everything coming together for good, will come and settle you down. It's wonderful what happens when Christ displaces worry at the center of your life." If something is on our minds, we don't need to try to push it out so we can pray about something else. God wants to hear about those things we're distracted by just as much as the other requests. We don't have the power to displace worry from the center of our lives, but God does.

FRUSTRATIONS INTO PRAYERS

Over the last few weeks, I've been intense—and that's putting it kindly. It's like I'm looking for a fight. My husband, Tyler, has been more patient with me than I deserve, and my kids love me something fierce. Still, my heart has been on the hunt for a reason to be frustrated. But one thing I've been learning recently is that when everyone around you seems extra annoying, it's time to pray. Not just for yourself, but for the people who are frustrating you. This will help you start seeing them the way God sees them. The Bible talks about praying for our actual enemies (Luke 6:28) and how that transforms our hearts. How much more should we pray for our families when we start to see them as the enemy? So I started praying for my three and thanking God for them, and it put me on a new path of gratitude and love.

QUESTIONS INTO PRAYERS

I believe the fear of the unknown is responsible for many people not fulfilling a call on their lives. We panic, afraid that we're heading the wrong direction, and the fear can be paralyzing. That's why every question mark we face needs to be redirected to the Lord. As you go about your day and feel the abrupt pause of not knowing what's next, lift it up to the Lord. Free yourself from having to figure it out on your own. We don't have to spiral down as we face negative thoughts; we can redirect our thoughts as we open our mouths and pray. Try praying the words of David in Psalm 143:8: "Show me the way I should go, for to you I entrust my life" (NIV).

I am always humbled by how quickly prayer can change things. My circumstances don't usually change on a dime, but the way I see them completely shifts as I commune with the God of the universe.

ACTION STEP

Write down one (or more) worries, frustrations, and questions, and turn them into prayers.

PRAYER

Father, give me wisdom and prompt my heart to pray when anxieties, annoyances, and unknowns start to take over. In Jesus' name, amen.

MORNING QUESTIONS

TAKEAWAY TODAY | *In what area of your life are you most in need of redirection right now?*

What can you do to remind yourself to pray when you're tempted to feel worry, frustration, or fear of the unknown?

DREADING TODAY | *Is there anything you're dreading today?*

REDEFINING TODAY | *If so, what is another way you can view that thing you're dreading?*

ASKING GOD TODAY | *What request are you bringing before the Lord today?*

EVENING QUESTIONS

REFLECTION | *How did your perspective change as you redirected your thoughts today?*

LITTLE VICTORIES | *Where did you see God show up even in small ways, reminding you that you aren't alone?*

WHITE FLAG MOMENTS | *When did you want to hide or escape today?*

MEMORY OF THE DAY | *What do you want to relish and thank God for?*

MY PRAYER

Day 26

MOB MENTALITY

WHEN YOU THINK OF a mob mentality, you don't immediately think of moms, do you? Me neither. But as I read about those silly old Israelites after God set them free from slavery in Egypt, I started to wonder if these two groups have more in common than I initially thought.

Exodus 16:2 says, "The whole congregation of the people of Israel grumbled against Moses and Aaron in the wilderness" (ESV). This is the reputation of the Israelites: grumblers and complainers. As I read this verse referencing the "whole congregation," I wondered if there were a few standouts who tried to fight the negativity. Was there one ray of sunshine who tried to start a different narrative? "Guys! We were *slaves* in Egypt! Sure, we're wandering the desert, but we were *slaves*! Why are we complaining about bland food and pretending we were better off in oppression? Let's give Moses and Aaron a break and see where this goes before we revolt."

Whatever the case, we don't hear about anyone with

countercultural thoughts. And knowing the story of Caleb and Joshua and how they viewed Canaan differently from their fellow scouts (Numbers 14), I assume Moses would have made mention of any opposing viewpoints.

We moms aren't wandering in the wilderness, but I see some similarities when it comes to the mob mentality. We live under an umbrella of misconceptions about motherhood. These lies often sound harmless, but if we buy into them, they can turn us into a herd of grumblers and complainers.

If you asked most people, this is what they'd say they know about moms: They wear yoga pants. They drive minivans. They don't sleep. They yell. They cry. They hide in bathrooms. They wish they could have pristine white couches or walls. They bemoan their bodies. They judge.

But it doesn't have to be this way. Okay, well technically, yes, all these things can be said of me, but they aren't going to *define* me. We know there's more to motherhood, and we aren't going to perpetuate the idea that this is all there is. Why? Because that's not what God intended for us. He has a better plan, and we don't have to slip into the mentality.

A. W. Tozer says, "We are not going to be sheep running over the precipice because other dumb sheep are running over it. We see the precipice—we know it is there. We are listening to the voice of the shepherd, not the voice of terrified sheep. The terrified, intimidated sheep are going everywhere."[9] I can't help but rejoice that we have a Shepherd who keeps us away from ledges. We just need to keep our eyes on him instead of following the lost herd. It turns out our best teacher on motherhood is a fella. Who knew? That God of ours is countercultural, as usual.

What if one person said no to grumbling? It wouldn't even have to be the whole herd. What if we started with saying no to just one misconception that's dragging us down today? What if we vowed to defy the voices of grumbling and complaining in our own heads and crowd them out with God's truth?

A grumpy moment is coming today—it's only a matter of time. But you can prepare yourself to reject it. Stand on the promise of 1 Corinthians 10:13: "No temptation has overtaken you that is not common to man. God is faithful, and he will not let you be tempted beyond your ability, but with the temptation he will also provide the way of escape, that you may be able to endure it" (ESV). We have a way out. We aren't helpless to reject the lies of this world. As you go about your day, I hope you will be empowered, knowing that we aren't destined for the herd. We have the power to stand out and follow the Shepherd.

ACTION STEP

Think of a typical moment when you would normally choose to go with the crowd. Write down what it would look like to defy the mob mentality of the grumpy mom, and commit to choosing a different path next time.

PRAYER

Father, I want your definition of motherhood, not the world's. I get caught in the herd mind-set so easily. Please give me the wisdom to see what doesn't align with you and the courage to go against the crowd and follow you. In Jesus' name, amen.

MORNING QUESTIONS

TAKEAWAY TODAY | *What do you typically hear moms grumbling about as part of the mob mentality?*

What kinds of things do you tend to complain about most?

DREADING TODAY | *Is there anything you're dreading today?*

REDEFINING TODAY | *If so, what is another way you can view that thing you're dreading?*

ASKING GOD TODAY | *What request are you bringing before the Lord today?*

EVENING QUESTIONS

REFLECTION | *Were you in any situations today where people were grumbling? How did you respond?*

LITTLE VICTORIES | *Where did you see God show up even in small ways, reminding you that you aren't alone?*

WHITE FLAG MOMENTS | *When did you want to hide or escape today?*

MEMORY OF THE DAY | *What do you want to relish and thank God for?*

MY PRAYER

TWO HANDS FULL

I HAVE TO SHARE A STORY that is embarrassing, not because it happened once, but because this has been a pattern for years. And it's one I'm just now noticing.

We sat on Vana's floor looking for a shirt that actually fit as I barked at both my girls to hurry up and get dressed. I was getting increasingly frustrated that they weren't following orders like a well-trained infantry and instead were acting like a total toddler and a baby (even though that's precisely what they were). I just wanted them to move faster, and I could feel my anger welling up with each minute that passed.

After a while I just couldn't take the tension inside me anymore. I wanted to identify the reason I was angry so I could replace it with truth. I had been here too many times to count, and the result was what felt like a never-ending slope of misfortune. First came the yelling. Then the tears. Then we were late. Then the car ride was just dreadful, and . . . you get the idea.

On that particular day, here's the lie I was believing: that I could do more than I needed to do and that my kids were supposed to keep up with my ridiculous pace. I believed that I could sloth around for an hour or two, distracted by my phone, instead of figuring out a game plan for the day. Then I decided we would take on the whole world on a Friday morning (you know, go to Costco, Home Depot, and Whole Foods, and find the perfect outfit for me for an upcoming event). As soon as my plan was formulated, I no longer had patience for the completely typical five minutes it takes Vivi to get her shoes on.

I had created a plan, albeit late in the game, and I expected that everyone had gotten the memo.

This was a pivotal moment for me. When I realized that my grumpiness was caused by the lie that I am a victim to busyness rather than one who is choosing busyness, I was able to relax. I was not going to make my kids suffer for my own choice to cram a lot into the morning. When I'm a victim to busyness, I see my children as bystanders who, if I go down, will go down with me. Maybe it's not that deliberate, but the end result is the same. If momma has to hurry, we all have to pick up the pace. But the truth is, I didn't have to hurry. I made that choice on my own.

Instead of feeling like a victim, I am trying to cling to Ecclesiastes 4:6: "Better one handful with tranquility than two handfuls with toil and chasing after the wind" (NIV). How full are your hands today? Maybe you've tried to cram more into a day than you should. If so, my bet is that this has led to yelling and frustration. And when it's all over, from my experience, the most depressing part is that all the striving turned out to be pointless.

I'm a go-getter, so having two hands full feels good and manageable—a way for me to reach my goals more efficiently. The problem is that this leaves no room for toddlers who keep pace with snails or for plans that get dismantled. It leaves no room for sickness and wardrobe malfunctions. What I think is the fast track is actually the very thing that's causing the journey to be painful. And ironically, it makes me feel behind even when I'm not.

Today, do you need to empty a hand? It may feel counterintuitive—and honestly, it still does to me. But it will transform us from moms who yell and scream into patient and grace-filled moms. We're going to be grateful for the results—and so will our kids.

ACTION STEP

If your plate is overflowing, ask God to reveal what might be toil or chasing after the wind. Commit to obey and empty a hand, regardless of what he asks you to surrender.

PRAYER

Father, I confess that I place some impossible demands on my kids sometimes, and my response when they don't perform up to my standards makes me someone I don't want to be. Give me wisdom and restraint to carry only what you've called me to handle for the day. Help me to release to someone else what is not mine to bear, or save it for another day. In Jesus' name, amen.

MORNING QUESTIONS

TAKEAWAY TODAY | *What impossible demands do you put on your kids?*

What would it look like to open your hand and release something that isn't yours to bear?

DREADING TODAY | *Is there anything you're dreading today?*

REDEFINING TODAY | *If so, what is another way you can view that thing you're dreading?*

ASKING GOD TODAY | *What request are you bringing before the Lord today?*

EVENING QUESTIONS

REFLECTION | *Were you able to let go of anything that was "chasing after the wind" today? What did that feel like?*

LITTLE VICTORIES | *Where did you see God show up even in small ways, reminding you that you aren't alone?*

WHITE FLAG MOMENTS | *When did you want to hide or escape today?*

MEMORY OF THE DAY | *What do you want to relish and thank God for?*

MY PRAYER

DOWN THE ROAD

WE TEND TO LIKE PEOPLE who look like us. It's easy to talk to the mom with kids the same age as ours, because we feel safe in commiserating over similar challenges. These relationships are important, because they remind us that the challenges of our days aren't unique to our own circumstances—they're just a natural part of motherhood. We find comfort in knowing we aren't the only ones awake at three in the morning with a baby who won't sleep.

But I think we need two other kinds of relationships as well. We need mentors, and we need to *be* mentors. We need someone further down the road, and we need someone who is a few steps behind us too. One has the power to challenge and motivate us, and the other can benefit from our experiences.

MENTORS
I remember hearing a speaker at a women's conference share Hebrews 13:7-8: "Appreciate your pastoral leaders who gave you the Word of God. Take a good look at the way they live, and

let their faithfulness instruct you, as well as their truthfulness. There should be a consistency that runs through us all. For Jesus doesn't change—yesterday, today, tomorrow, he's always totally himself" (MSG). She said that in her Bible she wrote down the names of women who have instructed her, and she prayed for women she could mentor in the same way.

I sometimes assume that moms who haven't had a toddler in thirty years are a bit out of touch with the way life is now—like maybe they've glamorized what a three-year-old is actually like. That's why I love this passage in Hebrews—it reminds me that the truths in God's Word are timeless, and we have much to learn from the generations that have gone before us.

When we seek biblical wisdom on mothering our kids, those truths that moms depended on thirty or even two hundred years ago hold true for us today. And there is something stabilizing about shifting our minds from the nuances of the day and focusing on the big picture. As I've been mentored by moms further down the road than me, I have been filled with hope and support to focus on the unchanging truths that will create a strong foundation for our family. Jesus doesn't change, and those mommas remind me of that reality.

We need our friends in the trenches, but we also need wisdom from moms who can help us see past the late nights and potty training—the ones who expand our perspective and lovingly remind us to soak up these days.

MENTEES

If we're being poured into, we can't keep it all for ourselves. Maybe you know someone who is journeying through pregnancy or taking her first newborn home from the hospital. What a privilege to get to encourage her with what you've learned on your own journey. In 2 Corinthians 1:4 we read that God "comforts us in all our troubles, so that we can comfort those in any trouble with the comfort we ourselves receive from God" (NIV).

Knowing that the things we've gone through can benefit others takes the sting out of hard situations in our past. We can see the purpose just a little bit more and gain confidence in the Lord's faithfulness. Our sense of gratitude increases too, whether because we're looking back on a particular season with fond memories or because we're thankful to be out of that particular hard stage. Any time we get to pour into someone else, we will be encouraged ourselves.

With mentors and mentees in our lives, we have countless opportunities for meaningful conversations—conversations that keep us focused on what's truly important. These relationships can help us in so many ways: by allowing us to focus on the big picture, by keeping us from wallowing in the day-to-day grime, by giving us an opportunity to serve and take our eyes off our own problems for a while, and by filling us with confidence. Thank the Lord, he did not call us to walk through motherhood alone.

ACTION STEP

Find a mentor and a mentee. This won't happen overnight, but start praying about it today.

PRAYER

Father, you created us for community, and that doesn't mean only with the moms who look just like me. Please help me to find a mentor to challenge and motivate me, and a mentee I can pour into and serve. In Jesus' name, amen.

MORNING QUESTIONS

TAKEAWAY TODAY | *What traits would you look for in a mentor?*

What do you have to offer someone you might mentor?

DREADING TODAY | *Is there anything you're dreading today?*

REDEFINING TODAY | *If so, what is another way you can view that thing you're dreading?*

ASKING GOD TODAY | *What request are you bringing before the Lord today?*

EVENING QUESTIONS

REFLECTION | *Have you thought of any women you might ask to be your mentor or mentee? What's one step you can take to initiate a conversation with them?*

LITTLE VICTORIES | *Where did you see God show up even in small ways, reminding you that you aren't alone?*

WHITE FLAG MOMENTS | *When did you want to hide or escape today?*

MEMORY OF THE DAY | *What do you want to relish and thank God for?*

MY PRAYER

Day 29

WHEN I'M MEEK,
I'M STRONG

TODAY WE'RE LEARNING about getting real quiet, y'all. And no, I'm not talking about hiding in the closet while we eat our kids' Halloween candy (although I wouldn't judge you for it!). Nope, today we're learning what it means to become meek and quiet—and about the unexpected energy that comes from that mind-set.

To the world, meek means weak, and quiet means lacking confidence. But to the Lord, these are traits of someone who finds their strength in him.

By this point, my Bible crush may be obvious: that dreamy Moses. I've already talked about his special connection with the Lord, but I haven't mentioned one important quality of his. Numbers 12:3 says, "Moses was very meek, more than all people who were on the face of the earth" (ESV). This verse caught my attention, because I came across it in the context of reading about the depth of Moses' faith. It didn't seem to fit what else we know about him as a person of strength.

I tend to downplay the importance of meekness, because the world's view—that meekness is synonymous with weakness—has seeped in and convinced me that meekness can't possibly be a source of strength. But as I've studied Moses more, I've started to see a man who walked with the Lord in a way most have never experienced. And I can't help but correlate his meekness with his deeper relationship with the Lord.

An attitude of meekness actually takes incredible strength. To willingly submit ourselves to the Lord's sovereignty and allow him to defend us and fight our battles takes more strength than it does to fight. The best part is that at the same time, meekness brings more rest.

As I started to piece together the correlation between meekness and rest, I stumbled on the perfect quote from A. W. Tozer in a chapter entitled "Meekness and Rest": "[The meek man] knows well that the world will never see him as God sees him and he has stopped caring. He rests perfectly content to allow God to set His own values. . . . In the meantime, he will have attained a place of soul rest. As he walks on in meekness, he will be happy to let God defend him."[10] Oh y'all! Does it sound glorious not to fight for things that ultimately don't matter? That means we no longer have to prove our value and make sure everyone knows how worthy we are. It means we can let the opinions of the world go in one ear and out the other without feeling like we have to continually do more to measure up. As we embrace this truth, we can let God's acceptance of us take up permanent residence in our minds.

I want to live in that perfect rest—the kind that isn't waiting for the world to validate what I'm doing. I think we all know that if we hold ourselves to the world's standards or do things for the praise of others, we will be worn out. But what hits me in a fresh way as I read Tozer's words is the starting point of that thought transformation. It all starts with meekness.

There are some things we can't change about the load we bear—the number of kids we have, the unique challenges they face, the financial strains we may be under. But there is something under our control: we can release all those unnecessary things we are piling in our arms that are adding to the weight—the things the world insists we should carry but that actually hold no value in God's eyes.

If we are unable to experience true rest, it's not because God is putting too much on us. It's because we think we are responsible for more than we truly are.

As we learn an attitude of meekness, we will free ourselves from feeling that the world needs us—and beyond that, we will stop caring about what the world thinks of us at all. Then we will find rest. Psalm 37:11 says, "The meek shall inherit the land and delight themselves in abundant peace" (ESV). How powerful the meek are, resting in the hands of the Lord.

ACTION STEP

Think of someone you know who displays true meekness. Make a list of qualities and actions they display that show their meekness, and strive to live out those characteristics this week.

PRAYER

Father, I want the kind of rest that comes from being meek. Change my heart, and help me to find rest in you. In Jesus' name, amen.

MORNING QUESTIONS

TAKEAWAY TODAY | *Does meekness come naturally for you? Why or why not?*

Why do you think meekness and rest are so closely connected?

DREADING TODAY | *Is there anything you're dreading today?*

REDEFINING TODAY | *If so, what is another way you can view that thing you're dreading?*

ASKING GOD TODAY | *What request are you bringing before the Lord today?*

EVENING QUESTIONS

REFLECTION | *Were there any moments today when you chose the path of meekness? What was the result?*

LITTLE VICTORIES | *Where did you see God show up even in small ways, reminding you that you aren't alone?*

WHITE FLAG MOMENTS | *When did you want to hide or escape today?*

MEMORY OF THE DAY | *What do you want to relish and thank God for?*

MY PRAYER

THAT YOU MAY KNOW

I'VE SPENT THE LAST several years encouraging prayer warriors to pray more. This is no easy feat in our busy world. And as if praying isn't hard enough, the part of prayer that requires *listening* through the noise feels nearly impossible. If your world is anything like mine, it's wall-to-wall giggling, screaming, and singing, leaving little room to hear a whisper from the Lord.

Despite how challenging prayer is, though, it's worth it. That's because hearing from God determines so much about how we walk through this life. In the story about Joshua in the battle for the Promised Land, we read these words spoken to him from the Lord: "Stretch out the javelin that is in your hand toward Ai, for I will give it into your hand" (Joshua 8:18, ESV). So Joshua stretched out his javelin toward the city.

What strikes me about this passage is that the Lord gave instructions to Joshua *in the middle of battle*, and Joshua heard him. I'd prefer to get all my instructions before the chaos begins. Maybe in my early-morning time, when the rest of the house is asleep. But the fact that the Lord spoke in the midst of the battle reminds me that he longs to speak to me in the chaos, too, not just in the quiet moments. And truth be told, most days that's when I need to be listening for him the most—when I'm in the middle of my daily battles.

Hearing God is life altering. When we're attuned to his voice, it can change the entire trajectory of our day. The question is, are we willing to listen?

Will we plow headfirst into destruction, or will we avoid the pitfalls of going our own way because we clearly heard the Lord redirecting us?

Will we believe the world's lies and face discouragement, or will we hear the Lord prompting us to embrace his joy instead?

Perhaps the most amazing thing about communicating with God is that he longs to reveal himself to us. I love finding patterns of repetition in the Bible. In the story about God sending plagues to Egypt to set the Israelites free, we see similar wording repeated six times in four chapters: "that you may know" and "you shall know." In each case, God is longing to reveal himself to human beings.

My guess is that you want God to reveal himself to you, too. Sometimes the evil one holds us back, and sometimes it's our own sin. But I'd venture to say that most of the time it's the pint-sized voices and the noble art of taking care of small humans that dull the voice of God. This might seem like a justifiable reason to ignore God, but he has a word for you today. He wanted the Israelites to know him even in the midst of challenging times, and that's what he wants for us, too:

- "that you may know there is no one like the LORD our God" (Exodus 8:10, NIV; see also 9:14)
- "you shall know that I am the LORD" (Exodus 7:17, ESV; see also 10:2)

- "that you may know that I am the LORD in the midst of the earth" (Exodus 8:22, ESV)
- "that you may know that the earth is the LORD's" (Exodus 9:29, ESV)

When we know how big God is, it helps us continue coming back to him. When we see him for who he truly is, we are less likely to see him as some pesky obligation and just one more person who wants our time and attention. As we see more of who he is through his Word, we recognize what a privilege it is that he longs to speak with us.

ACTION STEP

Set a timer for five minutes, and then lie on the ground on your back. With your hands up in the air, ask God, "What do you want me to do today, knowing you are Lord?" Chances are, you won't get a clear, audible response, but invite the Lord to speak anyway. When you rise, keep the same listening posture throughout your day.

PRAYER

Father, what an honor it is that you long to speak to me! I am humbled and overwhelmed by your love for me. I'm also embarrassed by how often I see spending time with you as an obligation. Please shift my heart and put a passion in me to find enough stillness in my days so I can hear you whisper to me. In Jesus' name, amen.

MORNING QUESTIONS

TAKEAWAY TODAY | *What tends to distract you from prayer and from hearing God's voice?*

Take a moment to ponder what it means that God wants to reveal himself to you. How does it feel to be pursued by the God of the universe?

DREADING TODAY | *Is there anything you're dreading today?*

REDEFINING TODAY | *If so, what is another way you can view that thing you're dreading?*

ASKING GOD TODAY | *What request are you bringing before the Lord today?*

EVENING QUESTIONS

REFLECTION | *Were there any moments today when you heard God's voice in the midst of the battle?*

LITTLE VICTORIES | *Where did you see God show up even in small ways, reminding you that you aren't alone?*

WHITE FLAG MOMENTS | *When did you want to hide or escape today?*

MEMORY OF THE DAY | *What do you want to relish and thank God for?*

MY PRAYER

Day 31

WAITING FOR A
QUIET LIFE

IN OUR PURSUIT OF PEACE, we usually assume that it's found on the other side of the chaos. Once we prune the schedule, cut the commitments, and declutter the house, we can calm down. This makes sense, but I've never managed to get to the other side of the chaos to find out. That's why I'm learning that peace is a mind-set rather than a result.

In the last few months, I've been in the thickest busy season of my life, and I've caught myself trying to postpone peace until my circumstances calm down. I'm discovering that peace is not a point we reach but a posture we carry.

When we see peace as a final destination, we respond in one of two ways: (1) We chalk this season up as a loss, take a backseat, and wait for peace to fall on us like a soft blanket. We are left feeling helpless, hopeless, and defeated when it doesn't happen. (2) We spend a lifetime with our shoulders up and our muscles tense, trying to hurry, hurry, hurry in an elaborate effort to get to finally reach peace. We end up feeling burned out, impatient, and discouraged as the victory line keeps moving right when we think we are about to reach it.

Either option relies on the idea that we can't experience peace amid chaos.

Author John Mark Comer says, "We think of peace as the absence of conflict, but God's heart for you is *shalom*. Complete peace *right in the middle of the chaos and noise and traffic of life*."[11] Praise the Lord! Right, momma? That means we don't need to ditch the kids to feel God's peace. And what's more, Comer continues, "The peace of God we are craving—gasping for—will show up in you, over you, around you, even as the winds of life are swirling around you like a tornado. It will guard you like a sentry, keeping you safe, not from suffering, but from anxiety."[12]

I have never really looked at peace like this before. I tend to see peace as the blessing that comes after I let go of anxiety, not something that *helps me* let go of that anxiety. I've seen it as the reward after the victory instead of the armor for the battle. I've seen it as the final destination, not the journey.

In the Lord's grace, not only can we find peace in the toddler years or elementary years or teenage years or whatever season of upheaval we are in, but that peace will actually be what protects us. How silly that I trade his peace for the world's definition!

There's a blessing in Numbers 6:24-26 that reveals more of God's view of shalom peace: "The LORD bless you and keep you; the LORD make his face to shine upon you and be gracious to you; the LORD lift up his countenance upon you and give you peace" (ESV). This may just sound like a nice prayer at first until we read it in the context of when it was said. This blessing was given to the Israelites by Moses' brother, Aaron, at a time when they were experiencing conflict with the nations all around them. I think the context here is as important as the blessing itself. Though the Israelites rarely experienced peace on the battle lines, they were able to experience peace in their hearts.

This is what God desires for all of us. I can stop waiting for peace to just show up one day, and I can start putting it on like armor for the here and now.

Right now, momma. Peace is for you right now.

So put it on. Suit up!

God never asked you to wait to experience peace in the ideal moments. He designed it to be experienced in the chaos of managing sibling squabbles and running late to appointments and whatever else you find yourself in the middle of on this very day.

ACTION STEP

Put on peace right now. It is going to take a shift in mind-set because we assume our circumstances have to change for peace to come. Reflect on the character of God and his promise for peace—and then accept it!

PRAYER

God, I want peace, but I only want your peace. I can feel my shoulders relax even as I put on your peace like armor, because I know this is what you have called me to. I have full faith that your peace will change my life. In Jesus' name, amen.

MORNING QUESTIONS

TAKEAWAY TODAY | *What feels like peace to you?*

In the past, what have you thought had to happen for you to experience peace? How does this new definition of peace change things?

DREADING TODAY | *Is there anything you're dreading today?*

REDEFINING TODAY | *If so, what is another way you can view that thing you're dreading?*

ASKING GOD TODAY | *What request are you bringing before the Lord today?*

EVENING QUESTIONS

REFLECTION | *Did you experience God's peace in the midst of your chaos today? Take a moment to thank him for his shalom.*

LITTLE VICTORIES | *Where did you see God show up even in small ways, reminding you that you aren't alone?*

WHITE FLAG MOMENTS | *When did you want to hide or escape today?*

MEMORY OF THE DAY | *What do you want to relish and thank God for?*

MY PRACER

NOTES

1. Jen Wilkin, *None like Him: 10 Ways God Is Different from Us (and Why That's a Good Thing)* (Wheaton, IL: Crossway, 2016), 33.
2. Elisabeth Elliot, *Discipline: The Glad Surrender* (Grand Rapids, MI: Revell, 1982), 101.
3. John Ortberg, *Soul Keeping: Caring for the Most Important Part of You* (Grand Rapids, MI: Zondervan, 2014), 20.
4. John C. Maxwell, *No Limits: Blow the Cap off Your Capacity* (New York: Hachette Book Group, 2017), 20.
5. Adapted from Brooke Castillo, *Self Coaching 101: Use Your Mind—Don't Let It Use You* (self-pub., 2009), 29.
6. Peter Scazzero, *Emotionally Healthy Spirituality: It's Impossible to Be Spiritually Mature While Remaining Emotionally Immature* (Grand Rapids, MI: Zondervan, 2006), 165.
7. Ortberg, *Soul Keeping*, 172.
8. Jennie Allen, *Anything: The Prayer That Unlocked My God and My Soul* (Nashville: Thomas Nelson, 2011), 59.
9. A. W. Tozer, *Culture: Living as Citizens of Heaven on Earth—Collected Insights from A. W. Tozer* (Chicago: Moody Publishers, 2016), 26.
10. A. W. Tozer, *The Pursuit of God*, updated edition (Chicago: Moody Publishers, 2015), 97.
11. John Mark Comer, *My Name Is Hope: Anxiety, Depression, and Life after Melancholy* (Portland: Graphe, 2011), 135.
12. Ibid.

ABOUT THE AUTHOR

VALERIE WOERNER is an author and the owner of Val Marie Paper, where her mission is to create practical tools and content that equip women to cut through the noise of everyday life and find fullness in the presence of the Lord.

Before starting Val Marie Paper in 2012, Valerie owned a wedding planning business and fell in love with paper design while creating wedding invitations for clients. During her first pregnancy, she created a prayer journal that she desperately needed—and she quickly found that many other women needed it too!

She graduated from Louisiana Tech University in 2007 with a degree in journalism and English. She thought she was destined to work for a big magazine in New York City but found she enjoyed personal column writing more. Her experience designing newspaper pages and her love for writing have come full circle, as she uses both to create content and products that encourage women to transform their lives through prayer and action.

Valerie lives in Lafayette, Louisiana, with her husband, Tyler, and their two daughters, Vivi and Vana. She loves reading, going on barefoot walks around her neighborhood, taking Sunday naps on her screened-in porch, and eating good Cajun food.

You can visit Valerie's shop at valmariepaper.com.

VAL MARIE PAPER

where prayer meets practical

PROMPTED PRAYER JOURNALS TO:
- ORGANIZE YOUR THOUGHTS
- ELIMINATE DISTRACTIONS
- DEEPEN YOUR FAITH

VALMARIEPAPER.COM